Mending Broken Children

Cognitive Ability Patterning for Successful Learning

Mending broken children

Cognitive Ability Patterning for Success

by Dr. Lloyd Flaro

Published by
LEARNING STRATEGIES GROUP INC.
Edmonton, Alberta
Box 44038
15505 - 118 Avenue
T5V 1N6

Published by Learning Strategies Group Inc.
Box 44038, 15505 - 118 Avenue
Edmonton, Alberta, Canada T5V 1N6

ISBN 0-921889-03-8

Editor-in-chief: Elizabeth McCardle
Editorial Assistant: Ann McLuckie

Cover Design: Vern Busby Advertising Design
Cover Illustration: Vern Busby Advertising Design
Typeset by Pièce de Résistant Ltée.
Printed by The Jasper Printing Group Ltd.

DEDICATION
This book is dedicated to my wife Marilyn,
for her support and encouragement; to my children,
Kristin and Melissa, who are always challenging
my presuppositions about how to learn.

TABLE OF CONTENTS

ACKNOWLEDGEMENTS

I wish to acknowledge:

The many learning disabled children who served as fine examples of people who can learn when given the appropriate strategies.

The many parents whose children I tested and taught the Cognitive Ability Patterning strategies. Feedback provided by them was essential for evaluating the effectiveness of Cognitive Ability Patterning.

All the teachers in St. Albert School District #3, who piloted some of my theories and models and gave me constructive feedback on their utility and productivity. Especial thanks goes to Emilie Keane who, as a resource room teacher and gifted education consultant, had the flexibility to find out what works. Special thanks needs to be given to Allanah Van Bryce and Sonja Layton, teachers of learning disabled students, who put the Cognitive Ability Patterning strategies into practice and didn't stop there. They integrated them with curriculum content and even other models to achieve good results with their learning disabled students.

Frank Josie, Director of Special Services, St. Albert Board of Education, District #3, who gave me leeway to conduct research on Cognitive Ability Patterning and to work directly with teachers to discover what did and did not work. He especially deserves thanks for getting me involved in presenting workshops to teachers which enabled me to obtain the necessary feedback to refine and develop this mode.

Dr Collins Meek, for his friendship, constant encouragement and editorial contributions.

Lisa McCardle, for her editorial genius.

Ann McLuckie, who typed the manuscript, revision after revision, and who, as a parent, offered valuable information about what should be in a book about learning disabled children.

Dr. Andrew Sereda, for his friendship, his willingness to share his knowledge about neurology and learning, and his support for this project.

Dr. Clifford Brown, developmental optometrist, who readily offered his knowledge about vision and learning disabilities and who consistently supported and encouraged me to the complete this manuscript.

Dr. Fern Snart, Faculty of Education, University of Alberta, who read the manuscript and offered valuable feedback.

Emile Mandin who supported and encouraged the development of CAP Strategies and who willingly tested them out.

The many other people who provided input and feedback about the contents of the book, but who have not been specifically mentioned outright in this acknowledgement.

Dr. Lloyd Flaro
April, 1989

FOREWORD

The field of learning disabilities is in an emergent and evolutionary stage. In fact, some evidence suggests that up to thirty per cent of the total school population could exhibit some form of learning disability — a sobering fact indeed!

Since the introduction of the term 'learning disability' in 1963, by Samuel Kirk, the concept has been developed and understood by professionals, who have brought their expertise to bear upon the elusive nature of this disturbing problem. They have focused upon its many facets: a child's perceptual-motor variables; social-emotional disturbance; neuropsychological variables, behavioral interventions for specific academic weaknesses; cognitive processing and models of information processing, and many more. Valid and important contributions to the assessment and remediation of learning disabilities have sprung from efforts in each of these areas.

However, one essential need of professionals who work on a day-to-day basis with learning disabled students is a resource that will help them integrate the existing wealth of information and translate it into practical ideas and suggestions. With *Mending Broken Children*, Dr. Flaro offers clear and concise descriptions of five current theoretical approaches within the field of learning disabilities. The reader reaches a subtle awareness that these approaches need not be mutually exclusive in our understanding of learning characteristics and potential learning difficulties in children. Dr. Flaro brings pertinent aspects of each theory to bear in an excellent integrative model of cognitive systems and processing styles in learning. Clarification through example is certainly a strength of the text.

The global nature of most definitions of learning disability necessitates that teachers and parents go several steps further in understanding the specific needs of any individual child. Dr. Flaro's book provides the basis for increased awareness of internal cognitive processes in learners, through careful attention to specific external behaviors. Again, the practical nature of the suggestions encompasses a strong theoretical base and an appropriate component of thoughtful commonsense.

Mending Broken Children presents sophisticated information to teachers and parents in a readable format, and is an excellent avenue for increasing observational, assessment and remedial skills. The book has great merit as a text for preservice teacher training, and as a resource for graduate courses in learning disabilities.

Dr. Fern Snart
Associate Professor
Educational Psychology
University of Alberta
Edmonton, Alberta, Canada

ABOUT THE AUTHOR

Lloyd Flaro, Ed.D., is a psychologist in full-time, private practice in Edmonton, Alberta, Canada. He is internationally recognized as a leader in the emergent field of learning disabilities.

For the past two decades, Dr. Flaro has been studying the problem of learning disabilities in students and has been searching for an easy-to-understand and applied process which teachers and parents alike could use to remediate students' learning difficulties.

During that time, he caught the first glimmer of the process which he would eventually call Cognitive Ability Patterning and which he would formulate for others to use in this his exceptional, ground-breaking book *Mending Broken Children*.

Dr. Flaro: "I believed then, as I do now, that children with learning disabilities have a lot to teach us about the workings of the mind, how over-specialization can limit our innate potential, and how different ways of thinking can become valuable resources in this age of change."

Dr. Flaro received his doctorate in Curriculum Development and Educational Psychology from the State University of New York at Buffalo in 1980.

PREFACE

In my medical practice as a neurological specialist, I have had the opportunity to assess many hundreds of children who have great difficulty with such basic academic skills as reading, spelling, and arithmetic. Unfortunately, many of these children face years of frustration, behavioral problems and low self-esteem before they are suspected of having a "learning disability."

Weaknesses in the basic academic skills adversely affect other subjects, and the children may adjust to the self-fulfilling prophecy of "slow learner." They may drop out of school, or be shunted into non-academic programs. Many are sent for medical and psychological assessment, often including a neurologic assessment.

Many of these children are hyperactive, have behavioral problems, and can't concentrate. Many are troubled with mood swings, headaches, and abdominal pain; especially when facing the pressures, frustrations and humiliation of constant academic failure.

For a time these children were labelled as having "minimal brain damage syndrome", largely because it was assumed there had to be something wrong with the way they processed information.

Employing some powerful new psychological techniques I learned from Dr. Flaro, I have gradually developed a different approach to understanding these children. I have come to the realization that children with learning problems are basically normal, but different. They have varying problems in their learning strategies, but there are common elements, which I considered to be critical. These children seem to have a different method of learning.

Using Dr. Flaro's techniques, I have observed that virtually all of these children have superior visualization skills, although they have difficulty recognizing and verbalizing letters and words.

Once a child's learning methods are understood, his or her learning strategy can be changed to overcome the learning obstacles. The problem is perhaps best considered a "learning difference" rather than a "learning disability."

By routinely employing Dr. Flaro's spelling techniques, I have demonstrated to parents and children that there is a tremendous capacity to learn and that the learning problem can be overcome, and once they realize the child is able to learn, a major step has been achieved in rebuilding the child's self-esteem.

This technique is only a small part of what is discussed in Dr. Flaro's excellent book. In my practice, I stress three major factors in the assessment and resolution process for learning problems:

1. Recognize that there is a learning problem, and the importance of obtaining help.
2. Bolster self-esteem by reinforcing the fact that, although a child may learn differently, he CAN learn. I frequently point out to parents and children some of the famous people who had similar difficulties when they were young. As the difficulties with reading, spelling and arithmetic are overcome, children can excel in academic pursuits such as fine arts, mathematics or physics (as did Einstein).
3. Realize the importance of diet; of avoiding additives, stimulants and refined sugar, and the addition of vitamins and minerals.

Dr. Flaro's book is a major contribution to the understanding of and effective solution to "learning disability" problems.

—Andrew Sereda, M.D., F.R.C.P. (C) Neurology
Edmonton, Alberta, Canada

INTRODUCTION

Children are as curious as they are individual. From almost the moment they are born, they seek to learn, to explore by touch and by sound, and then, as they learn their first words and form their first sentences, they begin to question. This search for knowledge and the rate at which a child learns is very much a part of each child's individual development. Each is a separate entity with his or her own special characteristics, albeit having many things in common with children of comparable ages. It follows that children may present the widest range of intelligence and experience, combined with great variation in their learning abilities and their temperamental reactions to the work of a class.

The modern tendency in all forms of education is to stress the necessity of developing each child as an individual, not merely as a fraction of an educational group. The center of gravity is placed in the living, active student. This emphasis on the development of individual minds and individual personalities must not overlook any of the obstacles that stand in the way of a child's individual development. Nor must it overlook the needs of any segment of the school population. Some children will progress rapidly and be successful students; others will find the road to knowledge more difficult because of learning obstacles, the nature of which is becoming increasingly clear.

This book addresses some of those obstacles - those learning disabilities that stand in the way of countless children today.

Most of the approaches and interventions used with learning disabled children are based on what is *wrong* rather than what is *right*. This position predisposes educators, teachers and parents to look for the things that a child cannot do rather than focusing on his strengths and assets. It was hoped that by studying successful and effective learners we could start to understand the internal cognitive operations and mechanisms underlying school learning and discover what the differences were between them and Learning Disabled children. The information gathered from these successful students in regard to their cognitive strategies and mental mechanisms was then explicitly taught to children with learning disabilities. The results were surprising, and very encouraging.

First, it became clear that many learning disabled students had similar internal capabilities to those of the more successful students, but simply did not know how to organize these into effective learning strategies. Second, whereas successful students knew when to apply a particular internal strategy, learning disabled students tended to use one learning strategy across all contexts. This meant that many learning disabled students did not learn to contextualize "content specific" learning strategies. These strategies, which operated *automatically* in successful children, had to be made to work as well for the learning disabled child.

Third, successful students had a variety of internal cognitive systems and strategies they could summon when needed. But, whenever the learning disabled student used his predominant learning strategy and it didn't work, he usually experienced frustration and failure. This experience of failing predisposed the child to develop belief systems that inevitably limited his potential for learning. Because he believed he couldn't learn, he developed perceptual "filters" which let in only those experiences that supported this belief. (This will be dealt with in a forthcoming book, tentatively titled *Mending Broken Spirits*, which will deal with the affective domain of learning disabled children.)

Finally, when learning disabled children were explicitly taught the successful strategies of the high achieving students, and specifically taught to use them appropriately, they seemed to learn exceptionally well. With practice, the strategies became automatic and functioned as well as their old strategies.

An interesting by-product of this successful experience became manifest: learning disabled children began to believe that they could learn! The experience of learning new cognitive strategies changed the learning disabled student's belief system about their capacity to learn. This would, and did, have great impact on their self-concept and self-worth.

Dr. Lloyd Flaro
Edmonton, Alberta, Canada
April, 1989

WHAT IS COGNITIVE ABILITY PATTERNING?

The term **Cognitive Ability Patterning** is rarely used in the text of *Mending Broken Children*. The lack of use is by commission, not omission, for the whole of the book is about Cognitive Ability Patterning and its various facets with respect to learning disabilities among the North American school-aged population.

The **process** of Cognitive Ability Patterning, however, needs to be made explicit for the reader at this point, for it is the framework upon which all my research has been based, and it also serves as the underlying structure for *Mending Broken Children*.

First and foremost, Cognitive Ability Patterning, or CAP for short, is the capturing of excellence and then making that excellence available to others.

Specifically, the Cognitive Ability Patterning process consists of eliciting cognitive strategies and mental modes of functioning from **successful** students. From the information gathered from those students about their cognitive strategies and mental mechanisms, learning formats are developed and then explicitly taught to students labeled learning disabled—with exceptional results. When learning disabled children were taught the successful strategies of the high achieving students, and taught specifically when to use them, they learned exceptionally well. In addition, a by-product of this successful experience manifested itself: the so-called learning disabled children actually began to believe that they could learn!

The approach taken in Cognitive Ability Patterning is to focus on the strengths of students. Most approaches and learning interventions used today with learning disabled students are based on what is wrong, rather than on what is right with the student. That approach predisposes teachers, educators and parents to look for the things the child cannot do rather than focusing on his or her strengths and assets. CAP focuses on the student's strengths and abilities thereby creating a positive learning environment and a successful and rewarding learning experience.

In North America, the problem of learning disabilities among our student population has reached epidemic proportions. Although the following statistic appears several times in *Mending Broken Children*, it bears repeating here: In the North American educational system, by the time students reach Grade 4 up to 30 percent of them have been labeled learning disabled!

Its comforting, isn't it, to think that none of us reading *Mending Broken Children* has ever had a significant learning disability—or have we? I believe we all have something to learn from *Mending Broken Children*. . . .

CHAPTER 1

RATIONALE AND RESEARCH BEHIND THE COGNITIVE ABILITY PATTERNING APPROACH

N INCREASING NUMBER of children in today's schools are being classified as learning disabled. Recent figures suggest that anywhere up to thirty percent of most school populations in the United States and Canada can be diagnosed as having a learning disability (Celdic, 1970; Lerner, 1981; Smith, 1983). Furthermore, 1 percent to 3 percent of our school students will be diagnosed as having such a severe learning disability that they will need special educational placement.

As a modest estimate of the prevalence of learning disabilities in our school systems, 3 percent to 5 percent is the most common figure cited by the leading experts (Farnham-Diggory, 1978; Johnson & Myklebust, 1967; Myers & Hammill, 1982; Sattler, 1982). This means that in an "average" school of 600 students, approximately 18 to 30 of those students will be designated learning disabled; and 3 to 18 students may qualify for the label, severely learning disabled. Obviously, the percentage in some schools could be higher or lower than these averages indicate.

These rising figures are probably the result of improved psychometric testing, diagnoses and early screening procedures. School counselors and school psychologists, better qualified in special education and testing, are doing a more competent job of identifying the child at risk. Similarly, a greater number of teachers have become cognizant of the characteristics frequently associated with learning disabilities, and as a consequence they are making more referrals as well as demanding more information about remedial procedures for learning disabled children.

Yet, what precisely is a learning disability? How can parents and teachers help the learning disabled child overcome his or her learning problems? What remedial procedures and educational programs are best suited to correct learning difficulties? Are there specific characteristics that can identify the learning disabled child? How can the teacher and the parent identify potential learning problems in young children?

Learning Disabilities: How Do You Know?

Although there are many definitions of learning disabilities, some so complex and abstruse as to cause cognitive congestion, learning disabled children can be defined educationally as those having significant difficulty in learning school-related subject matter such as reading, writing, mathematics or spelling. Excluded from this definition are children who are mentally retarded, emotionally or behaviorally disordered, or sensory impaired, unless they have a concomitant learning disability.

A number of investigators have offered more precise definitions of learning disabilities. Kirk (1962: 253) proposed the first major definition of learning disability, which prompted others to follow suit. He stated:

> A learning disability refers to a retardation, disorder, or delayed development in one or more of the processes of speech, language, reading, spelling, writing or arithmetic, resulting from a possible cerebral dysfunction and/or emotional or behavioral disturbance and not from mental retardation, sensory deprivation, or cultural or instructional factors.

Other investigators (Bateman, 1965; Kirk & Bateman, 1962; Myklebust, 1963 and 1968) have proposed various definitions of learning disabled and specific learning disabilities. Currently (1981), the definition proposed by the United States National Joint Committee for Learning Disabilities is in vogue:

> Learning disabilities is a generic term that refers to a heterogeneous group of disorders manifested by significant difficulties in the acquisition and use of listening, speaking, reading, writing, reasoning, or mathematical abilities. These disorders are intrinsic to the individual and presumed to be due to central nervous system dysfunction. Even though a learning disability may occur concomitantly with other handicapping conditions—for example, sensory impairment, mental retardation, social and emotional disturbance or environmental influences (cultural differences, insufficient/inappropriate instruction, psychogenic factors)—it is not the direct result of those conditions or influences. (Hammill, Leigh, McNutt, & Larsen, 1981, p.336).

In the United States, the current (1987) federal definition of learning disabilities (Federal Law P.L. 94142) states:

> Specific learning disability means a disorder in one or more of the basic psychological processes involved in understanding or in using language, spoken or written, which may manifest itself in an imperfect ability to listen, think, speak, read, write, spell,

or do mathematical calculations. The term includes such conditions as perceptual handicaps, brain injury, minimal brain dysfunction, dyslexia, and developmental aphasia. The term does not include children who have learning problems that are primarily the result of visual, hearing or motor handicaps; of mental retardation; of emotional disturbance; or of environmental, cultural, or economic disadvantage. (Federal Register, December 29, 1977.)

Recently, American and Canadian school boards have been empowered to develop special programs for learning disabled students. Within this mandate is also the power to define who is learning disabled. This means that whomever is classified as learning disabled varies from school district to school district, with each jurisdiction having the full power to define this amorphous entity.

Generally, learning disabled children possess average to better than average intellectual abilities. However, they do not achieve at the expected level of cognitive functioning. Rather, there tends to be a noticeable discrepancy between the learning disabled child's estimated learning potential and his or her actual school performance. This discrepancy may be perceived in the areas of language (written or spoken), spelling, mathematics, reading and writing. A discrepancy between expected potential and actual academic achievement usually indicates a learning disability if the student falls at or below the tenth percentile or has a grade equivalent score that is less than two-thirds of his or her current grade level. Frequently, however, a criterion of a one-year lag is the norm for Grades 1 to 3, while a two-year lag is set for Grade 4 and up.

Some students may have a discrepancy severe enough to prevent them from functioning in a regular classroom. These students are usually called severe learning disabled (SLD) and are placed in special educational programs designed to give them the necessary and appropriate remediation. Usually, these students are achieving at or below the second percentile in one academic area (reading, writing, arithmetic or spelling).

Theories of Learning Disabilities

Over the years, there have been many attempts to define the elements that constitute a learning disability. Various schools of thought have proposed theories to account for the causes of learning disabilities. These cover such diverse areas as: inner ear imbalances; biochemical imbalances, neurotransmitter deficiencies; psychosocial and socio-emotional factors; maturational lags; optometric difficulties, and many more. Generally, however, five theoretical approaches are used to explicate the nature of learning disabilities:

1. The Neurological Theory
2. The Information Processing Theory
3. The Maturational/Developmental Lag Theory
4. The Psychological Problems
5. The Vision Training Theory

1. The Neurological Theory

All behavior is the result of neurological processes. How the brain handles, organizes, codes and transforms incoming information predisposes children to learn and to think in vastly different ways. A mounting body of research has indicated that the left hemisphere processes information in a sequential, analytical, logical and step-by-step fashion. The left hemisphere seems to be the center for language abilities, determining our receptive and expressive capabilities. In contrast, the right hemisphere processes information in a simultaneous/holistic mode. It also houses such capabilities as visual-spatial skills, musical and artistic talents, and synthesizing capacities. The right hemisphere is activated by visual stimuli, whereas the left hemisphere responds more readily to linguistic inputs (Bogen, 1975; Chall & Mirsky, 1978; Gazzaniga, 1975; Ornstein, 1972, 1978; Rourke, Bakker, Fisk & Strang, 1983; Sattler, 1982; Wittrock, 1977, 1980).

How the brain processes and organizes information can be severely hampered by damage to the central nervous system (spinal cord and brain). Problems that interfere with the brain's processing capabilities can affect how a child learns to acquire knowledge. The neurological approach suggests that learning disabilities are the result of a "malfunctioning brain". In other words, something is interfering with the smooth operation of the brain's machinery. This could be the result of brain damage sustained, for example, by a blow to the head, involvement in a car accident, or the high fevers common to many childhood diseases. Some neurological problems may stem from prenatal complications, or may occur at birth (lack of oxygen to the brain, for example). However, a number of investigators believe that the earlier the neurological insult the more likely the brain may compensate for the dysfunction by setting up alternative neural pathways (Geschwind, 1985).

Research seems to indicate that approximately 15 percent to 20 percent of the learning disabled population have some form of neurological impairment. Some theorists, however, claim that *all* learning disabilities are the result of neurological dysfunction. This theoretical stance probably originated with the work of many clinicians who studied the cerebral behavior patterns of brain-damaged individuals. Isolating specific sites of damaged brain tissue seemed to correlate with the type of behavioral deficits exhibited by the those suffering brain damage. This finding led some researchers to hypothesize that the manifestations of such behaviors in learning disabled individuals were the same as those observed in the brain-damaged groups and therefore must represent underlying neurological dysfunctions. In many cases, however, there is no conclusive proof to substantiate the presence of neurological impairment in learning disabled children. Furthermore, the use of sophisticated technological equipment — Computerized Tomography (CT scan), Nuclear Magnetic Resonance (NMR), Positron Emission Tomography (PET scan) — has not been able to confirm the neurological approach conclusively.

Despite the inconclusive nature of brain research, to understand learning disabilities more fully, we must take into account the significant information offered. Due consideration should be given to the specialization of the cerebral hemispheres, the integration between them, and how an individual's ability to shift from one hemisphere to another, depending on the task demands, affects school learning. Indeed, understanding the structure and function of the brain can provide the school psychologist, the special education teacher and the interested parent, with a valid basis for discerning any one significant aspect of the nature of learning disabilities, and for developing remedial methods to correct such learning difficulties.

2. The Information Processing Theory

Cognitive psychology, or the information processing theory (Feuerstein, 1979, 1980), is concerned with the understanding and study of mental processes. More specifically, it is the study of subjective experiences; that is, it attempts to understand the cognitive variables and mental processes involved in learning.

Generally, the information processing approach views learning disabilities as reflecting a difference in how people organize, code and transform incoming stimulation (Bruner, 1967; Farnham-Diggory, 1978; Parnell-Burnstein, 1981). Thus, many learning disabled children's cognitive style (how they organize and process incoming information) may be inappropriate or inefficient to cope with the demands of the classroom. How a child attends, organizes and rehearses information may not match the task demands of the classroom nor meet the required educational outcomes. In a sense, there is a mismatch between the child's cognitive style and the task requirements of the school (Hunt & Sullivan, 1974).

The information processing approach suggests that learning disabled children need to be taught appropriate learning strategies. It focuses on teaching children how to think, how to solve problems, how to do inferential reasoning, and how to learn more efficiently within the classroom. The information processing approach attempts to identify the underlying cognitive mechanisms responsible for the learning problems or the behavioral deficits.

3. The Maturational/Developmental Lag Theory

This theory proposes that learning disabled children differ in their ability patterns and learning styles, with significant lags in some skills and strengths in others. Moreover, it suggests that the learning disabled child exhibits behaviors that reflect slow or delayed maturation in visual, motor, language and attention areas. Many of these skills form the basis for developing higher cognitive processes.

The notion that uneven patterns of development may be the causative element of some forms of learning disability is certainly evident in the well-known fact that girls develop at a faster rate than boys. Initially, girls exhibit greater verbal facility, language development emerges sooner, they talk earlier, and they are usually more mature when they start school. All this may be because boys' neural maturation in the cortical (brain) areas is slower to develop than that of girls. It explains why boys do less well at school than do girls in the earlier grades. It may also be the reason boys outnumber girls four to one in the incidence of learning disabilities.

Slower developmental/maturational rates of growth predispose learning disabled children to emulate younger children and to exhibit immature behaviors in the physical and mental domains (Kinsbourne & Caplan, 1979). Such children engage in behaviors that are more appropriate to those several years younger than themselves.

While developmental theorists realize that children grow at different developmental/maturational rates, the educational system seems unaware of this. All children are expected to perform in the same way and to learn the curriculum content without undue difficulty.

4. The Psychological Problems Theory

This approach proposes that some learning disabilities are the direct result of emotional or psychological disturbances. Psychological determinants set up emotional barriers that prevent a child from learning effectively within the classroom. Many classroom behaviors, such as poor academic performance, "acting-up", rebellious response, emotional outbursts, aggressiveness, negativism, social awkwardness, and others, may be the direct result of a learning disability, but many authors point to the underlying psychological dynamics as the real cause of such academic problems. The same authors cite research indicating that emotional disturbances will depress overall IQ scores on several intelligence tests, such as the WAIS or the WISC-R. The close relationship between affect and cognition leads many theorists to postulate emotional dysfunctions as the primary source of learning disabilities (Lerner, 1981; Ross, 1976; Smith, 1983).

Children react emotionally to stressful situations in their lives. Potential divorce, alcoholism, physical and sexual abuse, death in the family, or marital discord, may be contributing factors that affect poor school performance. For some children, this takes the form of misbehaving at school; for others, it means sacrificing school learning to the need for emotional and psychological survival. It is almost impossible to be an 'A' student when one is worried about whether or not one's parents are going to stay together. Sometimes the emotional impact of this type of stressful situation is so great that the student's marks drop dramatically. This obvious and rapid decline in academic achievement may be a sign of psychological disorder rather than a full-blown learning disability.

Usually, counselling (family or individual) is the recommended mode of treatment for children exhibiting learning dysfunctions because of underlying psychological or emotional problems. Until the psychological factors are treated and resolved, the learning difficulties will persist throughout the school years. If not addressed, these students may become school dropouts.

5. The Vision Training Theory

How important is the role of vision in learning? Does poor vision, or visual-perceptual deficiency, create learning disabilities? Do deficits in visual input systems decrease the efficiency of information processing systems and mental modes of functioning? (Davis, M., Whitner, 1982; Flax, N., 1972.) Vision theory proposes that visual and ocular efficiency are necessary skills for reading and other learning processes. In essence, impaired-visual input systems cybernetically affect the whole neuropsychological gestalt. In other words, input precedes output (Johnson & Myklebust, 1967). This hypothesis suggests that in order to develop cognitive visual processes, children must be able to attend to the visual aspects of their environment and then to internalize the informational feedback units into cognitive reference structures. Therefore, when children are learning to read or comprehend written text, they can use their past cognitive reference experiences to match or mismatch incoming information. In addition, they can elaborate upon instructional information by making verbal or visual associations inside their heads. Without the ability to take in information efficiently through the visual processing systems, children may not be able to develop internal visual processing systems. Moreover, they may decide to ignore the visual aspects of learning and concentrate on developing more sophisticated auditory and kinesthetic systems for processing, coding and organizing input stimuli. While there is controversy about the effectiveness of vision training, behavioral optometrists adamantly postulate two assumptions underlying their theory: (1) vision is learned; and (2) it is trainable and modifiable. Keogh and Pelland (1985:229) state that:

> . . . behavioral optometrists see efficient visual functioning as a critical component in development, and believe that many learning problems can be traced to an inadequate developmental foundation in basic skills. Thus, behavioral optometrists advocate training programs developed to enhance the eyes' ability to move, align, fixate, and focus as a team.

Behavioral optometrists have developed a variety of techniques designed to increase visual efficiency; that is, functional integration of the processes involved in coordination of visual motor and vision capabilities. The training program includes such techniques as tracking and pursuit skills, vectrographs, lenses, glasses and prisms (Huxley, 1942; Kraskin, 1973; MacDonald, 1962-1965; Roby, 1983; Schrock, 1968-1972).

In summary, there are many reasons for learning disabilities. A learning disability is not a unitary entity; many factors can be responsible for its occurrence and, in this sense, all five approaches have something useful to contribute to our understanding of learning disability.

Identification and Prediction of a Learning Disability

The identification of the learning disabled child should begin in kindergarten. Unfortunately, few school districts employ any type of screening procedure designed to detect a child who may be at risk or who could develop potential learning problems later on in school. Preschool screening devices and early school assessment procedures are relatively nonexistent in many school districts because of general disagreement among theorists as to what exactly constitutes a learning disability. Ross (1980) states it much more succinctly: "The field of learning disabilities is long on theory and short on fact."

Be that as it may, research provides parents, teachers and counselors with some potentially useful predictors that seem to be highly correlated with academic success. These predictors, which follow, represent the abilities of a child entering Kindergarten and Grade 1:

1. the ability to name the letters of the alphabet
2. the ability of the child to recite the alphabet in the proper order
3. auditory discrimination of sounds in words
4. copying geometric designs
5. the ability to name pictures

6. vocabulary comprehension
7. visual discrimination abilities
8. numbers knowledge
9. the ability to follow directions.

Lack of these predictors can, but not necessarily will, predispose children to develop learning disabilities. Of utmost importance, the teacher's and the parents' observations of the developing child need to be taken into consideration during any screening procedure. Observations of visual, motor, linguistic or auditory skills can provide the examiner with vital information regarding a child's cognitive, educational and social competencies.

Research suggests that teachers and parents can note certain characteristics in children that may identify a child with a potential learning problem. In general, the following characteristics appear more frequently in children with learning problems: short attention span; hyperactive motor activity; impulsiveness; inaccurate counting; mirror writing; reversal of letters and numbers; language difficulties (delayed speech development, poor speech); psychomotor difficulties, such as poor coordination or the inability to copy figures; achievement low in some subjects and high in others; memory deficits; poor reading ability; emotional liability; poor impulse control; destructiveness; expressive difficulties; acting as if not hearing; responding differentially to sounds; word finding difficulties or difficulties in naming objects; following directions poorly; inability to follow classroom instructions; poor concept of time; and difficulty in verbalizing thoughts. The preceding is not by any means an exhaustive list, and if you have concerns about your child, then do contact your nearest Association for Children and Adults with Learning Disabilities for more detailed information. A child will need extensive psychometric testing before anyone can be reasonably sure that that child has some form of learning disability.

Special Educational Placements for the Learning Disabled Child

If a child is found to exhibit characteristics of a learning disability, and psychometric testing confirms the observations, then he or she may need to be placed in a special educational program. This depends, of course, upon the severity of the diagnosed learning disability as well as the child's overall academic performance. Many learning disabled children can function within the regular classroom with supportive remedial and resource room help. In such a case, the learning disabled child would leave the regular classroom each day for a specified period of time. In the resource room, the child would be provided with special remedial programs designed to correct the cognitive deficits by teaching him more efficient learning strategies. For instance, some learning disabled children need to be taught directly how to gather relevant information about a particular problem, or how to organize material appropriately. However, it should not be inferred that all students attending remedial classes are learning disabled. This simply is not so.

Severely learning disabled students have special educational needs and may not be able to function in a regular classroom until their learning problems are remediated through special class placement. Usually, these learning disabled students are placed in a special classroom where they can receive one-to-one instruction, and the remedial teacher can design an individual learning program suited to the needs of each child. Special instructional techniques and pedagogical approaches are employed to alter or modify how the learning disabled child codes, organizes and transforms classroom material. As the learning disabled child makes academic progress, he will be integrated into the regular classroom stream.

Currently, there is a great deal of controversy about the overall effectiveness of special classes and resource rooms for learning disabled students. A number of investigators have challenged the educational and remedial effectiveness of programs, special classes and resource rooms for the learning disabled, arguing cogently that many of the educational interventions do not work (Brown, Kiraly & McKinnon, 1979; Dunn, 1968; Gordon & Poze, 1978; Hammill, 1972; Lerner, 1981; Myers & Hammill, 1982). However, these same authors realize the potential effectiveness of special programs and resource rooms, and attribute overall success to the quality and expertise of the resource room teacher. Further, they credit the success of remedial programs for learning disabled children to the teacher's flexibility in meeting the educational needs of children with a wide range of learning difficulties.

To make resource rooms and special classes work, the teacher must have a solid understanding of the underlying cognitive and neuropsychological processes involved in efficient and productive learning. Not only must the teacher understand how the child processes, codes and organizes incoming information, he must realize that each individual student thinks and learns differently. As well, that teacher needs to be able to identify *how* children think, *what* internal cognitive systems are being used to learn, and *why* they are not learning from regular classroom instruction. This will be covered in Chapter 2.

Suggested Exercises for Parents and Teachers

What is it really like to have a learning disability? The term learning disabled is used casually, yet no one, including many experts, knows precisely what it is or how to treat it. Conceptually and pragmatically, we know that some children cannot learn in certain subject areas (mathematics, spelling, reading, writing, for instance); but what does it *feel* like to be unable to learn how to do something? What must it *be* like to know, without a doubt, that every time you engaged in a particular task or skill, you couldn't do it, no matter how hard you tried or how motivated you were?

Exercise One

Try this simple experiment, for which you will need a hand mirror, a sheet of paper and a pencil. Hold the mirror against the edge of the paper, then, using your dominant hand (right hand in most people), write your first and last name by looking only at the letters as they appear in the mirror. The only feedback you may use is the visual information you are receiving via the mirror. Once you have mastered this skill, try it again, but this time with your nondominant hand! The first exercise will give you an idea of the frustration some children with learning disabilities are constantly going through, but the second exercise will give you a more intense awareness of what it is like to be learning disabled!

Exercise Two

Using your mind's eye, imagine that you have just learned the function of a doorknob. You have learned its shape, what it feels like, and how, if you turn it, you can open a door. You have experimented with how it feels, what it looks like, and even how it sounds when you turn it. Then, as you leave this intriguing gadget, you suddenly develop amnesia. You forget what a doorknob is, and how it looks and works! Soon, you encounter another doorknob, and you wonder what this strange and interesting object is. As you study it and try to solve its mystery, you do so with an eerie feeling of *déja vu* — a sense of having seen this puzzle before.

Imagine then, what it would be like to interact in an environment (say, a classroom) wherein something you had only just learned had gone from your mind. You would wander aimlessly around, without a compass to guide you, and if your teacher asked you to recall some part of the lesson, you wouldn't know what to say, because you wouldn't have the slightest idea of what was expected of you.

Learning disabled students with memory deficits approach each learning task as if it is something new, something they have never seen before - as, indeed, to them it is! This is tantamount to learning the same things over and over and over again. And who has not experienced the frustration of a gramophone needle that is caught in a groove and the record plays the same piece over and over again until someone corrects it. This is the world of the learning disabled child!

Exercise Three

Find an adult partner willing to participate in the following exercise, explaining that your objective is to gather some information about how he or she does certain things. Tell him that this exercise is designed to help you understand how learning disabled students learn. Once he has agreed to participate, explain that you will ask him to do certain things inside his head, while you will attempt to find out what cognitive processes he uses in thinking about the assigned task. Ask him to spell the words psychology, planetarium, equestrian, and liaison. When he has spelled the words, even if he does so incorrectly, ask *how* he was able to spell them. That is, what went on inside his head? Once you have determined *what cognitive processes were used*, ask yourself if they are the same strategies you would use. You can extend this exercise by having individuals work on mathematical calculations, define certain words, or solve problems.

This particular exercise is designed to prepare you for Chapter 2. By becoming aware of how external behaviors are correlated with internal cognitive processes, you will begin to perceive patterns that seem connected to learning excellence, as well as those patterns that consistently operate in learning disabled children.

CHAPTER 2
MAPPING THE INNER WORLD OF THE LEARNING DISABLED CHILD

OW THAT WE HAVE SOME definitional conception of what constitutes a learning disability, we need to develop a model for understanding how the learning disabled child processes, encodes, organizes and transforms incoming information. In order to map the inner workings and psychological mechanisms of the learning disabled child's mind, we need to explore the important areas of learning and cognitive styles within the information processing theory. We also need to examine hemispheric styles within the neurological theory. In this way, the reader can begin to understand an important premise, repeated throughout this book—that most learning differences are the natural by-product of how an individual perceives and thinks.

Learning/Cognitive Styles

Several researchers (Atwood, 1975; Basbe & Swassing, 1979; Dunn & Dunn, 1975, 1979; Hunt, 1970, 1974; Lawrence,1982; Murphy & Brown, 1970) have written extensively about matching teaching styles to a student's preferred learning style or preferred sensory system. The basic premise underlying this approach is that the student has a preferential style for processing and inputting information. For maximum learning to occur, the teacher should present the instruction in a way that will match the student's preferred learning style. The closer the fit, the more likely it is that the student will understand the instructional material.

To date, the research on learning styles is controversial. Some investigators (Levine, Brooks & Shonoff, 1980; Rosner, 1979) deny the usefulness of the concept of learning styles, claiming that most research in this area suffers from methodological errors. While an individual may choose to input information through a preferred sensory system or modality (seeing, hearing, feeling, touching, tasting or smelling), it does not provide us with any information about the cognitive systems the individual employs to code, organize and transform that information. Learning styles do not tell us what is going on inside the individual's head.

Figure 1

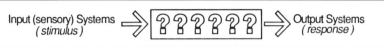

The learning styles paradigm in Figure 1 resembles Skinner's (1953) stimulus and response model which ignored the internal mental processes the individual used to represent informational or environmental stimulation. This was pejoratively referred to as the "blackbox phenomena."

Sensory perceptual (input) channels represent an individual's predisposition to favor one modality system for "taking in" information. The individual is biased to pay attention to certain aspects of the environment while ignoring other modality properties. This is illustrated in the following example. In several workshops, I use this exercise to develop the concept of preferred input channels. Participants are asked to make a circle by joining the thumb and index finger of their right hand, and then to "Place the circle on your chin," while I demonstrate by placing my own thumb and index finger against my cheek! Faced with this incongruent message, most participants respond with their preferred systems, then, as they look around and observe the different responses, they laugh and express amazement at the manner in which each has interpreted the instruction.

Although the research on learning styles is controversial, consider what happens to a young child who prefers to input information/ instruction through the visual modality. Generally, this child may not attend to the teacher's verbal instructions, seeming to be easily distracted by extraneous (visual) events. This child will probably ask for the instructions to be repeated, much to the teacher's annoyance. However, when the instructions are presented visually (written on the blackboard), the same child has no trouble in completing the assigned task. Interestingly enough, many children who do prefer a visual input channel are often referred for complete audiological examinations, with a high percentage of the referrals being negative.

While learning styles represent one part of the total learning process, other types of cognitive mechanisms are employed to expand and elaborate upon the incoming instruction and information. These organizing, encoding and transforming internal psychoneurological processes are generally referred to as *cognitive styles*: relatively stable and consistent ways in which an individual organizes, perceives and conceptualizes information. In effect, cognitive styles refer to how the individual thinks and processes information; that is, they refer to the types of information processing strategies used to code and organize incoming information into meaningful schematic structures.

Generally, the basic premise underlying the concept of cognitive styles is that individuals (in this case, students) process information in cognitively different ways.

Recent research on hemispheric specialization and cerebral lateralization (Chall & Mirsky, 1978; Das, Kirby & Jarman, 1979; McCarthy, 1980; Segalowitz, 1983; Williams, 1983; Wittrock, 1980) has made us more aware that individuals do process information in different ways. Each hemisphere seems to possess a different mode of thinking: a different cognitive learning style. The hemispheric specialization model will be discussed more thoroughly in the section on hemispheric styles (see page 18).

While a number of investigators were developing theories about the nature and cause of cognitive development in children (Almy, 1966; Elkind & Flavell, 1969; Flavell, 1963; Hunt, 1961; Inhelder, Sinclair & Bovet, 1974; Qiaget, 1951, 1952, 1964), Jerome Bruner's investigations (1960, 1966) more directly addressed the area of cognitive styles: how children learn to think. Bruner (1960) focused primarily on the questions: How does the child know something? How does the child make sense out of the impinging stimuli bombarding his sensory receptors? What are the structural components and cognitive operations involved in efficient learning? How do we know what kind of representation the child has "inside his head"? And, even more important, how can we identify the internal mechanisms and cognitive operations that may be responsible for learning dysfunctions?

Each of us thinks differently. Bruner's research (1960, 1964, 1966) began to delineate the psychological mechanisms and the cognitive processes responsible for idiosyncratic thinking styles. His findings suggested that some children represented incoming information by transforming the input stimuli into pictorial representations of what was seen, heard or felt. His subjects literally coded information in terms of images or pictures.

Further investigation revealed other sensory-modality coding mechanisms involved in the organization of incoming information into different cognitive structures. Some children represent input enactively, through kinesthetic (movement and body sensation) cognitive systems: they respond to input data in terms of internal feelings or external body sensations. This theoretical position corresponds isomorphically to Piaget's (1966) stage of sensori-motor development, the first stage of cognitive growth. The child gathers information about his environment by touching objects, through frequent manipulations of things, and by interacting kinesthetically with the environment. The child literally absorbs the environment by taking it apart, intensely manipulating it, and then (one hopes) putting it back together. This interaction with the environment allows the child not only to gather information but, at the same time, provides the basis for him to develop sensory schemas (mental representations).

In a sense, one could postulate that these primitive investigative interactions are the beginnings of a cognitive map of a child's world.

Similarly, Bruner (1966) hypothesized that some children represent information symbolically by using language and inner speech to guide their external behaviors (Luria, 1982; Sokolov, 1975; Vygotsky, 1962). Initially, children use external speech to identify the environment. Many children, for example, talk out loud to themselves, verbally labelling or classifying their environment into simple to complex categories prior to speech becoming internalized. Once speech is internalized, children use an internal monologue or dialogue to represent the incoming information. More specifically, they employ verbal mediation strategies to encode and to transform environmental stimuli (Camp, 1977; Meichenbaum, 1971, 1977). Luria (1978) postulates that inner speech is the result of frontal lobe activity. Inner language appears to be the prerequisite for the ability to plan and to anticipate consequences.

While some knowledge is represented in terms of inner language and/or self-talk, higher-order cognitive functions may be represented through symbols such as numbers, letters or abstract conceptualizations (Cassirer, 1970, 1974). This symbol system provides us with new perceptions about our world, allowing us to live in a new dimension of reality. Mathematics, for example, is a highly sophisticated system of symbols that has enabled us to develop revolutionary theories about the nature of our world.

Bruner's research on cognitive growth and development suggested that children employ certain cognitive behaviors, self-talk, visualizations and visceral sensations, to organize and transform incoming information. Further investigations not only confirmed Bruner's earlier findings, they also correlated with external behaviors and indicated that there were definite patterns of consistency in children's preferences for one system over another. In Bruner's (1966:49) own words: "What is remarkable about the long series of experiments . . . is not only that there is considerable consistency in these preferences for one or the other modality, but also that many *features of behavior become correlated with the preference*" (emphasis added).

Similarly, other investigators (Lerner, 1976; McCarthy, 1980) developed theories and procedures based on the concepts of preferred cognitive systems for organizing and transforming incoming information. Lerner (1976: 171), for example, observed that "children appear to have one optimal perceptual modality for learning." The striking similarity between Lerner's conclusion and that of Bruner is obvious.

While Bruner realized the importance of knowing how the child processed information, he concluded that (at this stage of his development) representational systems or cognitive behaviors might be inferred from observations of external behavior. Although he understood the necessary step of learning to index covert cognitive processes based upon the examination of overt behavioral responses, Bruner (1966), at that time, did not have a method for connecting the two. Interestingly enough, Bruner was on the right track when he observed that internal cognitive behaviors could to some degree be indexed based on the words that children used to discuss how they thought they learned. He noted that children who exhibited a preference for representing information visually also used visual words to explain how they were processing and organizing incoming information. The children who organized input data in terms of visual pictures or representations used a visual vocabulary to tell others how they learned something, how they remembered particular concepts, and how they solved problems. Similarly, children who employed auditory or kinesthetic cognitive systems seemed to have a corresponding preference for the words they used to explain their own internal cognitive processes.

Neurolinguistic Programming: Elaborations on Bruner's Theory

Neurolinguistic programming (NLP) not only elaborates upon Bruner's concept of representational thought, it also explains how individuals represent incoming information and experiences into specific cognitive sensory systems. On the basis of the type of representational system or preferred cognitive style they employ in their thinking, individuals develop conceptual maps or schemas for guiding their behavior in the contexts of learning, thinking and understanding. The concept of representational system (cognitive style) is employed by Bandler and Grinder (1975) to explain the processes involved in assimilating information into one's consciousness. Dilts (1980:17) explains:

> The basic elements from which the patterns of human behavior are formed are the perceptual systems through which the members of the species operate on their own environment: vision (sight), audition (hearing), kinesthesis (body sensations) and olfaction/gustation (smell/taste). The neurolinguistic programming model presupposes that all of the distinctions we as human beings are able to make concerning our environment (internal and external) and our behavior can be carefully represented in terms of these systems. These perceptual classes constitute the structural parameters of human knowledge.

We postulate that all of our ongoing experience can usefully be coded as consisting of some combination of these sensory classes. In our previous work we have chosen to represent and abbreviate the expression of our ongoing sensory experience as a 4-tuple. This 4-tuple is shown visually as $(V^{ei}, A^{ei}, K^{ei}, O^{ei})$. Here, the capital letters are abbreviations for the major sensory classes or representational systems that we use to make our models of the world. . . .

The superscripts 'e' and 'i' indicate whether the representations are coming from sources external to us, as when we are looking at, listening to, feeling, smelling or tasting something that is outside of us, or whether they are internally generated, as when we are remembering or imagining some sound, feeling, taste or smell. . . .

In NLP, sensory systems have much more functional significance than is attributed to them by classical models in which the senses are regarded as passive input mechanisms. The sensory information or distinctions received through each of these systems initiate/modulate, via neural interconnections, an individual's processes and output. Each perceptual class forms a sensory-motor complex that becomes "response-able" for certain classes of behavior. These sensory-motor complexes are called representational systems in NLP.

Each representational system forms a three-part network: (1) input, (2) representational/processing, and (3) output. The first stage, input, involves gathering information and getting feedback from the environment (both internal and external). Representation/processing includes the mapping of the environment and the establishment of behavioral strategies such as learning, decision making, information storage, and so on. Output is the causal transformation of the representational mapping process.

We will see, later on, that the concept of representational systems as preferred modes for organizing incoming information has rather important implications for understanding learning disabilities. To understand learning disabilities fully, we must consider the specialization of the hemispheres, the integration between them, and the individual's ability to shift back and forth from one to the other in the appropriate learning context.

Hemispheric Specialization

A substantial amount of evidence has shown that each cerebral hemisphere is predisposed to process information in distinctly different ways (Bogen, 1975; Chall & Mirsky, 1978; Gazzaniga, 1975;

Ornstein, 1978; Wittrock, 1980). The cerebral specialization model postulates that each hemisphere has a unique and special style of processing information; each has a particular cognitive style for handling and organizing input data.

Certain functional differences have been attributed to each cerebral hemisphere (Table 1). Many research studies have concluded that each cerebral hemisphere tends to respond selectively to various input stimuli. To a large degree, each hemisphere cognitively processes information differently. The left hemisphere is characterized as logical, rational and analytical, while the right hemisphere is perceived as nonrational (emotive), intuitive and metaphorical. The left cerebral cortex responds more efficiently to verbal-linguistic inputs, whereas the right hemisphere reacts more strongly to visual or tactile inputs.

The hemispheric cognitive style of the left cerebral cortex is characterized as sequential (or serial). This verbal label represents the left hemisphere's ability to process information in a linear, step-by-step fashion. It breaks large units into smaller, discrete, digestible parts. This "chunking down" process permits causal analysis, relational inferences and inductive processes to be brought to bear on the input stimuli.

While the left hemisphere employs an analytical-sequential cognitive style for understanding information, the right cerebral cortex operates by synthesizing all the parts into whole configurations or patterns. This simultaneous mode of integrating discrete bits and pieces of informational units into larger, more coherent, cognitive chunks may provide the basis for higher level thinking skills (de Bono, 1967, 1969).

Various abilities have been associated with each cerebral hemisphere. Mathematics, writing, reading and language have been placed in the domain of the left hemisphere. Music, art, drawing, and movement are believed to be the logical products of the right cortex.

Kaufman (1980) has developed an intelligence test (the *Kaufman Assessment Battery for Children*) to determine the different cognitive styles (sequential *vs* simultaneous) each individual child uses to solve problems. By determining a child's most preferred hemispheric cognitive style, the educator could use the child's strengths to teach him more effective ways to learn the required subject matter.

According to Kaufman (1980), the sequential learner solves problems best by mentally arranging the small cognitive/informational units in a consecutive, step-by-step fashion. The sequential learner operates by manipulating information in a successive serial order. On the other hand, the simultaneous learner solves problems best through synthesizing the parts into whole patterns or configurations. The simultaneous learner can integrate many pieces of information at the

---

TABLE 1
Posited Characteristics of
Each Cerebral Hemisphere

Left Hemisphere	Right Hemisphere
• serial processing	• parallel processing
• one-at-a-time	• all-at-once
• sequential processing	• simultaneous processing
• inductive reasoning	• deductive reasoning
• detects features, then looks at whole	• detects gestalts, then looks at details
• analytical, logical; it sees causes and effects	• relational, constructional, pattern recognition
• temporal	• spatial
• produces linear thinking	• produces imagistic thinking
• chunks down	• chunks up
• verbal; is expressed in words	• visual-spatial; it uses images
• has the power of syntax, the grammatical ability to string words together	• has limited syntax but responds to words as images
• can remember complex motor sequences	• can remember complex images or visual gestalts
• good at remembering names	• good at remembering faces
• responds best to a phonetic approach	• responds best to a slight word approach
• verbal	• nonverbal
• responds best to a sight word approach	• responds best to visual inputs
• primarily associated with right-eye movement	• primarily associated with left-eye movement
• logical	• intuitive
• parts/segmented	• holistic/gestalten
• analytical	• creative
• focal	• diffuse
• abstract/symbolic	• concrete
• rational thought	• emotional thought

---

same time or in parallel fashion.

For instance, in the area of reading comprehension, the sequential learner, having read a particular story, will be able to describe the sequence of events that occurred throughout the story, but he may not know what the overall theme or meaning of the story is all about. Conversely, the simultaneous learner will know what the story is about; he will grasp the overall meaning of the passages in the story, but may not be able to delineate the sequence of events that took place.

In mathematics, the simultaneous learner may solve a problem and obtain the correct answer but be unable to say how he arrived at it! The sequential learner will be a favorite of many teachers, because he will solve problems by applying the correct formula or set of

Figure 2

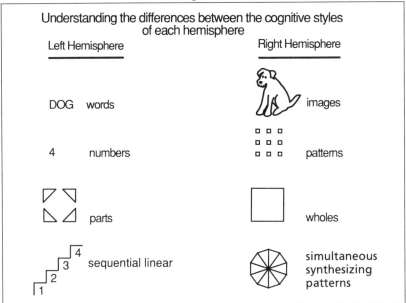

Understanding the differences between the cognitive styles
of each hemisphere

Left Hemisphere   Right Hemisphere

DOG   words   images

4   numbers   patterns

      parts   wholes

      sequential linear   simultaneous
                                   synthesizing
                                   patterns

procedures taught by the teacher. This type of student learns best by using a cookbook approach to solving problems, and he will be able to tell you step-by-step how he arrived at the answer.

Sequential processing seems to be important in letter-sound associations; learning basic arithmetical facts; memorizing lists of spelling words; remembering specific rules such as those in grammar; following rules and sorting problems into their component parts. On the other hand, simultaneous processing seems especially important for interpreting the overall meaning of a story; recognizing the shape and orthographic features of letters and numbers; comparing and evaluating incoming information; and solving problems by visualizing or imagining ("image-ing") them in their entirety.

Obviously, both cognitive and hemispheric styles are involved in most problem-solving situations. However, many individuals seem to be overspecialized in one style, almost to the exclusion of the other. This is certainly evident in learning disabled students who struggle in some subject areas but are competent in other academic areas. Some learning disabled students seem to be overly proficient in the simultaneous mode of cognitive processing, and particularly weak in the sequential processing style. Such students will probably have difficulties with word attack, decoding and phonics skills, or in remembering the sequence of a story. Similarly, they may not be able to chunk down larger cognitive units into smaller discrete pieces that would allow them to attack the problem with smaller "bites."

Simultaneous learners with weak sequential abilities may find it difficult to express their thoughts in words or be unable to write their thoughts on paper.

The learning disabled student who is overly specialized in sequential processing but deficient in the simultaneous learner mode may experience difficulties in the areas of sight-word recognition and identification; reading comprehension in the sense of understanding the overall meaning of a story; comparing and evaluating; and using and understanding diagrams, charts or maps. Similarly, these same students may not be able to synthesize component parts into higher levels of cognitive organization.

Let's apply the hemispheric specialization model to the task of learning the alphabet. For most children this is relatively simple, requiring the process of sequencing the letters in the proper order. Yet, the overly specialized sequential learner may learn how to recite the letters in the proper sequence but at the same time not know which letter comes after "L" without starting at the beginning and going through the whole sequence of letters again! For the student to remember which letter follows another, he will need to visualize the letters in the appropriate sequence. Without this simultaneous-visual cognitive process, this student will without doubt have difficulty with the following assignment:

    1. c d e _ _ _
    2. m n o _ _ _
    3. p q r _ _ _

The sequential learner relies solely on a verbal-auditory approach to learning. This approach employs verbal mediation strategies or auditory rehearsal methods to learn facts and concepts. The verbal-auditory processor (sequentializer) learns best through repetition of the facts; he repeats the letters to himself rather than visually understanding the relationship among them. This child would probably have tremendous difficulty finding the missing pieces in the following alphanumeric sequences:

    1. c 3 d 4 _ _ _ _
    2. 5 _ 6 _ _ g 8

As another example, the auditory-verbal learner will learn basic computation facts through counting inside his head, by an auditory rehearsal. In many cases, the sequential learner employs his fingers to mark off each digit or repeated number. This procedure permits him to solve a problem like $6 + 8 = 14$ by the laborious employment of finger manipulations and verbal-auditory procedures. However, once the student obtains the correct answer, if you ask him what $8 + 6$ equals, he will again resort to his fingers to get the correct answer! Inside his head, he has not employed the visual processes associated with a simultaneous mode and consequently *does not see the relationship* between the two equations. In Piaget's (1960) terms, he has not developed the concept of reversibility. Perhaps this ability is a function of a simultaneous-visual process rather than being tied to any developmental stage of cognitive development.

A Conceptual Model for Understanding How Children Learn

We know that different children prefer different input channels for "taking in information" just as we know that many individuals have preferential cognitive and hemispheric styles for organizing, transforming, encoding and recoding environmental stimulation. What we don't know at this point is how to identify a child's preferred input and cognitive systems for acquiring knowledge. Bruner's (1966) contemplations on the ability to identify the internal mental cognitive systems based on external behaviors provide a basis on which to proceed. What we need to discover are patterns of behavioral responses that are associated with neural transforms and that are consistently correlated with internal mental operations and cognitive systems.

The diagnosis of learning problems and the provision of effective remedial procedures are dependent upon the development of a conceptual model that explains how the proposed internal psychological mechanisms work. The model must also predict the type of learning problem that could arise as a result of the dysfunctional operation of the postulated internal cognitive structures. Finally, external behaviors will be perceived as the logical product of the postulated internal structures or, more technically, the logical consequences of neural transforms. Such a model suggests that any product or performance deficiency will be the logical by-product of information processing system dysfunctions or cognitive strategy deficits.

The general conceptual model presented in Figure 3 is in the incipient stage of development. It does, however, integrate various findings from the research on cognitive and metacognitive psychology, the brain sciences, the neurolinguistic programming paradigm and the field of cybernetics. The model offers educators, teachers, psychologists, special educators and others a systematic method for conceptualizing learning disabilities. It provides a conceptual basis for diagnosing a learning disability at the various levels: input, cognitive systems and output.

At the *input level* we are not only concerned about the relative intactness of the perceptual sensory systems but also with the preferential predisposition of the child to favor one sensory system

Figure 3

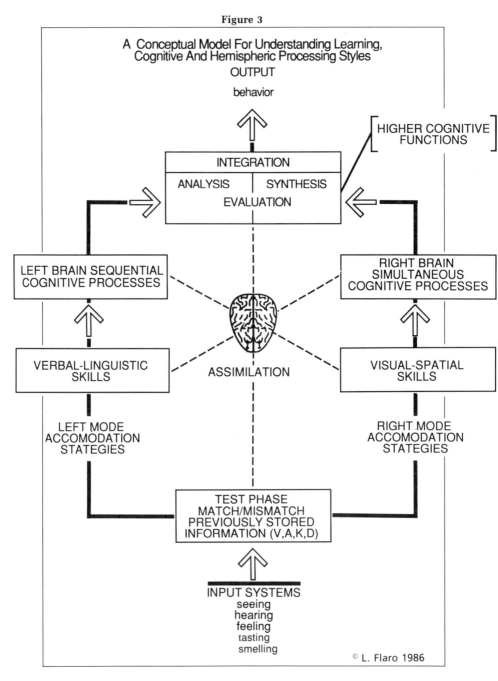

A Conceptual Model For Understanding Learning,
Cognitive And Hemispheric Processing Styles

OUTPUT

behavior

HIGHER COGNITIVE
FUNCTIONS

INTEGRATION

ANALYSIS | SYNTHESIS

EVALUATION

LEFT BRAIN SEQUENTIAL
COGNITIVE PROCESSES

RIGHT BRAIN
SIMULTANEOUS
COGNITIVE PROCESSES

VERBAL-LINGUISTIC
SKILLS

ASSIMILATION

VISUAL-SPATIAL
SKILLS

LEFT MODE
ACCOMODATION
STATEGIES

RIGHT MODE
ACCOMODATION
STATEGIES

TEST PHASE
MATCH/MISMATCH
PREVIOUSLY STORED
INFORMATION (V,A,K,D)

INPUT SYSTEMS
seeing
hearing
feeling
tasting
smelling

© L. Flaro 1986

at the expense of the other cognitive systems. In preferred learning,
styles affect learning.

After receiving the sensory inputs, how is the information

processed, organized, encoded and transformed to permit the child to make sense out of the sensory registration? The model postulates that all sensory systems are first processed through a test system that matches or mismatches the incoming information with previously acquired knowledge (Miller, Galanter & Pribram, 1860). This feed-forward mechanism and template-processing system produces assimilatory or accommodatory cognitive processes depending on whether the input information matches or mismatches previously acquired knowledge. In other words, if the environmental stimulation or input information does not match with stored knowledge, this difference or disequilibrium propels the organism to engage in accommodatory cognitive processes. Usually the disequilibrium propels the unmatched information to be recoded either in terms of verbal-linguistic or visual-spatial processes (Figure 4).

If the information is subjected to a verbal-linguistic investigation or recoding, then the functional properties of the left hemisphere are brought to bear upon the problem. The left hemisphere's sequential abilities are employed to provide a basis for further analysis until some verbal code or category is found that will recode or recategorize the information. The child will use a verbal-auditory cognitive system to process the information in an attempt to break it into smaller cognitive chunks that can be matched to an existing knowledge structure.

On the other hand, if the information is fed through the visual-spatial information processing system, the functional properties of the right hemisphere operate upon the mismatched information. This would entail the process of integration and synthesis of all component parts until some larger pattern or recognizable gestalt emerges as a means of connecting the unmatched information to other cognitive structures or the formation of totally new levels of cognition. Both assimilatory and accommodatory processes are more fully represented in Figure 4.

In many cases, the unmatched input is fed through both cognitive systems simultaneously, with the most proficient one providing the appropriate response. The integration of the verbal-linguistic and the visual-spatial cognitive mechanisms provides the means for the student to develop generative learning systems (Wittrock, 1980); or the ability to learn how to learn, based on the combined efforts of both cerebral hemispheres.

As an example of how the model in Figure 4 works, let us discuss the process of spelling. The teacher asks the student to spell the word "Albuquerque." The student hears the verbal-linguistic input and responds by accessing past acquired knowledge systems to determine if he knows how to spell the word. If he does, he EXITS by either vocally reproducing the correct sequence of letters that constitute the

Figure 4

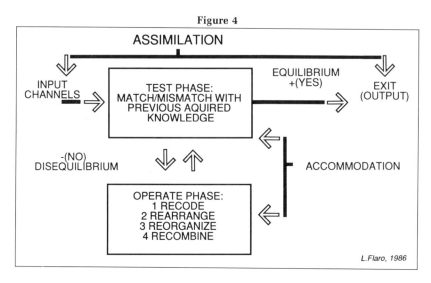

word "Albuquerque", or he writes it down on paper. On the other hand, if the word is not in his cognitive lexicon, the student OPERATES accommodatively by attempting to develop a PLAN for spelling the unknown word. If the student prefers a verbal-linguistic hemispheric style for decoding words, then he will apply the rules of phonics to sound out the word. As he sounds out the letters he may construct sequential images of the word until he obtains a sequence of letters that sound just right, such as "Allburkirkkey." This creates an equilibrium/congruence and the student exits by producing (motorically/vocally) the constructed series of letters. It is important at this point to realize that the student may EVALUATE the correctness of the word solely on the basis of phonetic analysis.

Similarly, the child may employ the visual-spatial cognitive system to determine the correct spelling of the word "Albuquerque." He may use a sight word knowledge base to obtain segmented gestalts of the word (for example, 'All') or he may compare the sounds of the word with previously known and visually intact words. He will then search his visual lexicon to look for similar sounding words until he finds one that appears right. Once he has accessed a visual image of how the word should be spelled he exits. Again, the student probably will EVALUATE the production of the word, but this time it will be in accordance with how the word looks.

In many cases, where the word triggers no internal representation in either the verbal-linguistic or the visual-spatial cognitive systems, both hemispheres collaborate to produce the best possible rendition of the word. The verbal-linguistic system may translate the appropriate sounds while the visual-spatial system constructs holistic images to match the incoming sounds of the required task. However, several possible cognitive transforms can be generated to solve the spelling problem. This dilemma would entail the integrative stage where the spelling productions are evaluated for accuracy as well as for the most likely choice. This evaluation will be based on the integration of analytical and synthetic cognitive processes. If overspecialization is evident, then the dominant hemisphere will have evaluative priority over the less dominant one.

In summary, the input stimulus is received via a sensory registration system where the input stimulus is matched against existing knowledge structures and past learnings. If the word is assimilated (matched with other cognitive systems), equilibrium occurs and the organism exits. When the word cannot be assimilated, this difference propels the organism to engage in accommodatory cognitive processes. Thus, either the verbal-linguistic or visual-spatial cognitive processes are brought to bear upon the incoming stimulation. Other possibilities exist in this model to explain spelling behavior. However, the example serves to illustrate the complexity of the underlying psychological mechanisms as well as to demonstrate the need for an integration of all cognitive systems to produce efficient responses.

Indexing Cognitive Systems

Bruner's investigations (1960,1966) produced several working hypotheses: (1) learning is a function of how a child thinks; how a child represents incoming information; (2) children code/process incoming information through sensory perceptual cognitive systems, enactive, iconic and symbolic; and (3) there seems to be a consistent set of behavioral patterns that correlate reliably with the child's internal cognitive processes or information processing strategies.

While Bruner (1966) proposed that the words a child uses are indicative of the internal cognitive processes or information processing strategies engaged in problem solving, other researchers (Bakan, 1969, 1971; Bandler & Grinder, 1977; Day, 1976; Dilts, 1977; Duke, 1968; Kinsbourne, 1974, 1972) have suggested that other external behaviors, such as head tilts and eye movements, are indicative of cerebral lateralization.

Words and Cognitive Processes

Bruner's (1960,1966) observations of children's thinking styles led him to conclude that the words children use are reflections of cognitive processing. Children who preferred a visual modality for processing information had a tendency to use visual words to express their thoughts. More recently, Bandler and Grinder (1976) and others (Owens, 1977; Peale, 1980; Shaw, 1977) have found a positive correlation between the words individuals use and the representational (cognitive) systems activated to process task-specific questions.

The importance of understanding how words are related to the internal processing systems is a prerequisite step towards comprehending the nature of learning disabilities. The visual learner will use words like see, show, look, watch, clear, picture, imagine, visualize and focus, to provide the educator with information about how he is thinking. The auditory learner will employ words such as hear, sounds like, tell, say, clicks, loud, soft, or discuss; while the kinesthetic learner vocalizes words such as feel, in touch, get a handle on, grasp, strike, hit or stuck. The words the child vocalizes and expresses as part of his vocabulary are not figurative representations but literal translations of the internal cognitive systems being orchestrated to learn. Words can, therefore, be employed by teachers to index internal cognitive behaviors (see Table 2 for a more comprehensive list of possible words and phrases).

While words can be incorporated as part of the diagnostic procedure to identify internal cognitive behaviors, it is also important to realize that how the educator employs words to explain concepts or to teach facts may impact on the student in a negative way. To have the child repeat the words to himself while using visual images to learn concepts creates a substantial mismatch between the demands of the environment and the cognitive behaviors involved in his learning. Thus, the educator should attempt to employ sensory-specific words to explain concepts or to teach facts such as those in Table 2.

On many occasions, I have heard teachers ask students to pay attention to the words or to think about the problem, without providing any sensory-specific information about how to do it. Usually, one of two things happens in this situation. The child may employ his most preferred sensory system to organize, code and transform the requested task, which may be in total opposition to what the teacher is asking of him. If the teacher, for example, suggests that the student employ a "sounding-out" approach to decode the word and the child attempts to decode it visually, a mismatch is created that can affect future learning. Or, the child may decode the instruction to pay attention in terms of the context. If the child has learned to solve such tasks through phonics, without consideration of a visual/sight-word approach, he will continue to employ the strategy he believes the teacher wants in that context.

Most of the problems discussed above occur as a result of using unspecified words to give instructions to students. As teachers and educators, we tend to fall back on terms we believe others already know (take the words used in this book as an example). Moreover, we sometimes forget that the way we organize and process information is not necessarily that used by others. When someone doesn't

TABLE 2
Representational System Words and Preferred Cognitive Styles

Visual	Auditory	Kinesthetic	Unspecified
look at	hear	feel	think
see	say	touch	figure out
watch	sound	grasp	understand
describe	talk	warm/cool	aware
picture	tell	gets a handle on	know
imagine	clicks	struggle	learn
visualize	tone	stuck	remember
focus in	pitch	dislike	recall
focus on; view	rings a bell; strikes a chord	mad/sad/glad; grip	learning disability
viewpoint	discuss	tactile	gifted
perspective	comment	hot-headed	slow learner
visual	verbal(ize)	step-by-step	respect
colorful	expressive	hand-in-hand	shy
black and white	wordy; talkative	tense up; anxious	non-verbal; dyslexic
perceive clearly	audio; tell myself	active; moving about	enrichment; perception
clarify, flash	clarify, state	strike/hit; massage	remediation
insight	deaf	depressed	
go blank	auditory	kinesthetic	
mind's eye	listen	in touch	
eye-to-eye	earful	get a grip on	

understand what we say, we have a tendency to become upset, annoyed and frustrated. On many occasions, we may even wonder, unfairly, about the intellectual capabilities of the other person!

Eye Movements and Cerebral Lateralization

A number of investigators (Bakan, 1969, 1971; Day, 1964; Duke, 1968: Ehrlichman, Weiner & Baker, 1974; Kinsbourne, 1972, 1974; Kocel, Galin, Ornstein & Merrin, 1972; Thomason, Arbuckle & Cody, 1980) have concluded that the direction of eye movement is related to the cerebral hemispheres: left-eye movements are reflective of right-hemispheric cognitive processes, while right-eye movements activate the cognitive systems of the left hemisphere.

Day (1964) obtained results suggesting that individuals do exhibit characteristic eye-movement patterns, that eye-movement behavior does occur in response to differential questioning, and that children do not seem to develop stabilized and characteristic eye-movement patterns until they reach the age of three.

Similarly, Duke (1968) investigated whether eye movements occurred more frequently in response to factual questions or reflective questions. He found that his subjects exhibited greater eye movements in response to reflective questions. Kinsbourne (1972) replicated this study by presenting subjects with verbal, numerical and spatial questions. The results showed that in right-handed subjects there was consistently more right-eye movement in response to verbal questions and more left-ocular movement in response to spatial questions. This supports the hypothesis that eye movements are indicative of cerebral lateralization. In Kinsbourne's study, however, no consistent eye movement was detected in response to numeric queries.

Further research by Bakan (1969) suggests that left-eye movers out-perform right-eye movers on appositional cognitive tasks; left-eye movers report more vivid and lucid internal imagery correlated with right-hemispheric functions. Left-eye movers also consider themselves to be more musically inclined than right-eye movers; right-eye movers seem to be more competent in propositional cognitive processes, which is substantiated by the fact that they receive higher scores on the SAT sub-tests. Similarly, Hartnett (1974) has postulated that an individual's hemispheric style may play a critical role in second-language learning. Right-eye movers would tend to employ an analytical, deductive method for learning a second language, whereas left-eye movers may learn the intonation and rhythmic patterns or nonverbal components of a second language. This study presupposes that right-eye movers employ a different cognitive style than left-eye movers. The right-eye mover would tend to use an analytical, logical approach while the left-eye mover would use a relational, holistical cognitive mode to learn.

Based on the research in the brain sciences, Bandler and Grinder (1977) hypothesized that the direction in which an individual moves his eyes is indicative of the cognitive style operating at that moment. Eye-movement behavior, therefore, provides the observer with information about the representational system or conceptual style being used by the individual. While their generalizations about eye-movement behavior seem unscientific, the fact that no other researchers have implicated horizontal as well as vertical ocular movements as potential indices of cognitive processing, seems somewhat parochial. A number of investigators (Andreas, 1983; Beale, 1980; Beck & Beck, 1984; Cole-Hitchcock, 1980; Conway & Siegelman, 1983; Dorn, 1983; Ellickson, 1981, 1983; Flaro, 1986; Hernandez, 1981; Mace, 1982; Owens, 1978) have now begun to take the Bandler and Grinder hypothesis seriously and although many studies support the Bandler and Grinder (1977) hypothesis, some findings question it. Closer inspection of these studies, however, shows serious errors in methodology as well as a significant lack of understanding the conceptual-theoretical basis underlying the eye-movement hypothesis.

The generalizations surrounding eye-scanning behaviors are

Figure 5

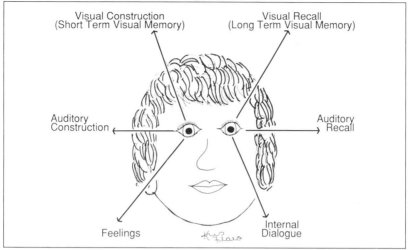

Visual Construction
(Short Term Visual Memory)

Visual Recall
(Long Term Visual Memory)

Auditory
Construction

Auditory
Recall

Feelings

Internal
Dialogue

presupposed to reflect a person's underlying cognitive styles and therefore will be considered a useful index in identifying the individual child's cognitive systems. Clinical experience and research (Flaro, 1986) support the utility of eye-movement observation and substantiate its diagnostic value in understanding the learning disabled student. Further research (Flaro, in press) suggests a strong correlation between eye-movement behaviors and performance on the verbal and performance sub-tests of the *Wechsler Intelligence Scale for Children - Revised* (WISC-R). There is also some evidence to suggest that eye movements can be used as predictors of overall performance on the WISC-R, and in the identification of verbal performance discrepancies.

According to Bandler and Grinder (1977), the direction of horizontal, lateral or vertical eye movement is reflective of underlying cognitive processes and hemispheric styles (see Figure 5). A normally right-handed student who moves his eyes up and to the left in response to a question or verbal instruction is accessing past images or pictorial representations associated with previously acquired knowledge. He is remembering what Haber (1969) referred to as eidetic images. The student who looks up and to the right when answering a query is constructing pictures of things he has never seen before - like a pink elephant with zebra stripes. Upper-right quadrant eye movement activates the left cerebral (visual) sequential functional properties of the contralateral (opposite) hemisphere.

Conjugate lateral eye movements reflect auditory processing. Lateral eye movement to the left represents past auditory tape loops such as nursery rhymes, jingles and nonverbal sounds. It is also associated with auditory memory. Right-eye movement is associated with the process of auditory construction; the process of putting one's thoughts and experiences into words. Downward eye movement indicates the use of internal dialogue or inner speech. This means that when a student who is right-handed looks down and to the left he is talking to himself. For example, when you ask a student to spell "nature" he may look down and to the left in order to sound it out. In many cases, this downward left-eye movement is accompanied by mouth motions or external subvocalizations.

Ocular movements downward and to the right indicate kinesthetic processing: feelings. This seems to be a spot favored by depressed people as well as learning disabled students. When a poor speller is asked to spell something, he tends to look down and to the right and may verbalize the feeling that he cannot do it. Some individuals, Wayne Gretzky for instance, have a tendency to look straight up. When you listen to their words with respect to what is going on, they literally "see it" using visual-motor processing.

There are some individuals who, when asked any type of question, seem able to look straight ahead without any apparent eye movement, yet they are able to recall facts, concepts or numbers. However, a close look at the pupils of their eyes shows that they dilate or contract, and usually, if asked what they were doing internally, they respond that they were making pictures or talking to themselves. Further investigation seems to indicate that large, dilated pupils are correlated with visualization. However, the visualization the individual describes seems to be projected externally of themselves. Similarly, constricted pupils seem to be associated with internal dialogue or internal kinesthetic sensations.

These eye-movement patterns are generalizations about the nature of internal processes. Clinical experiences and research studies support eye movements as potentially reliable measures for indexing internal processing strategies and internal cognitive styles. With this information about eye-movement behaviors, word usage, representational systems and preferred learning modalities, the remedial and resource teacher can begin to develop procedures to correct various learning problems. This will be discussed throughout the rest of the book.

Suggested Exercises for Parents and Teachers

Are you a sequential thinker or a simultaneous thinker? Do you prefer a visual, auditory or kinesthetic cognitive system for organizing, encoding, transforming and translating incoming information? When engaged in conversation, do you tend to employ more visual, auditory or kinesthetic words? Are you more of a right-eye mover or a left-eye mover? Or are you the digital type who uses unspecified words and usually looks straight ahead? What follows is a series of quizzes that will give you some information about how *you* learn things and how *you* process incoming information. The quizzes are intended to give you an experiential base for understanding the content of Chapter 2. They are designed to assist you in learning about yourself, so that you can begin to identify the learning styles and cognitive systems of your students and children. They are also structured to give you some insight into how you think, know and understand environmental stimulation and verbal instruction.

Quiz One
Understanding Your Personal Learning Style.

1. When you are studying an unfamiliar topic or subject, do you:
   - ☐ a. prefer to gather information from many subject areas?
   - ☐ b. prefer to stay fairly close to the main topic?

2. Would you prefer to:
   - ☐ a. know a little about a great many subjects?
   - ☐ b. become an expert/specialist in just one subject?

3. When you read a textbook, are you a person who:
   - ☐ a. skips ahead and reads chapters of special interest out of sequence?
   - ☐ b. works systematically from one chapter to the next, not proceeding until you have understood the material you have read thus far?

4. When you are eliciting information about some subject of interest to you, do you:
   - ☐ a. tend to ask broad and general questions that call for a general response?
   - ☐ b. tend to ask narrow questions that demand specific answers?

5. While browsing in a bookstore, do you:
   - ☐ a. roam around looking at books on a wide variety of topics?
   - ☐ b. stay more or less rooted to one place, focusing your attention on just a couple of subject areas?

6. Are you best at remembering:
   - ☐ a. general information or principles?
   - ☐ b. facts?

7. As teachers and parents, do you think that educators should:
   - ☐ a. give students exposure to a wide variety of subjects?
   - ☐ b. spend a lot of time on one subject area so that students can learn a great deal about their specialties?

8. When you are learning something new, do you prefer to:
   - ☐ a. follow general guidelines?
   - ☐ b. work to a detailed plan of action?

Interpretation

If you score more than five 'a's you are more inclined toward being a simultaneous learner. Five or more 'b's and you are more of a sequential learner. This test is meant as a self-awareness exercise, not one that strictly categorizes you.

Quiz Two
Are you right-brained (R), left-brained (L), or integrated (I)?

1. Are you better at:
   - ☐ a. remembering faces?
   - ☐ b. remembering names? or are you
   - ☐ c. equally facile at both?

2. Do you respond best to:
   - ☐ a. verbal instructions?
   - ☐ b. visual/kinesthetic instructions? or are you
   - ☐ c. equally responsive to both sets of instructions?

3. When taking a test or examination, do you prefer:
   - ☐ a. multiple choice questions?
   - ☐ b. essay type questions? or are you
   - ☐ c. equally good at both?

4. When you solve a problem, do you prefer:
   - ☐ a. to solve it in a logical, sequential manner
   - ☐ b. to get the overall concept first? or do you
   - ☐ c. have equal preference?

5. Are you:
   - ☐ a. good at thinking up humorous things to say and do?
   - ☐ b. poor at thinking up humorous things to say and do?
   - ☐ c. moderately good at thinking up humorous things to say and do?

6. Do you:
   - ☐ a. prefer kinesthetic stimuli (movement and action)?
   - ☐ b. prefer auditory, verbal stimuli?
   - ☐ c. have equal preference for kinesthetic and auditory stimuli?

7. Do you:
   - ☐ a. use examples and metaphors when you talk?
   - ☐ b. occasionally use examples and metaphors when you talk?
   - ☐ c. never use any examples and metaphors when you talk?

8. Do you prefer:
   □ a. mathematics?
   □ b. art?
   □ c. music?

9. Do you remember better when a teacher or person uses words to:
   □ a. explain things to you?
   □ b. describe things in visual terms?
   □ c. does both of the above?

10 Do you:
   □ a. get lost easily?
   □ b. find your way around even in strange places?
   □ c. get lost sometimes and sometimes find your way around?

Answers

1. a. R (Right-brained)
   b. L (Left-brained)
   c. I (Integrated)

2. a. L
   b. R
   c. I

3. a. L
   b. R
   c. I

4. a. L
   b. R
   c. I

5. a. R
   b. L
   c. I

6. a. R
   b. L
   c. I

7. a. R
   b. I
   c. L

8. a. L
   b. R
   c. I

9. a. L
   b. R
   c. I

10 a. L
   b. R
   c. I

Score
Left-brained _____ ; Right-brained _____ ; Integrated _____

CHAPTER 3
COGNITIVE PROCESSING DIFFERENCES

IFFERENT LEARNING environments need to be recommended for youngsters with divergent modes of processing information: a structured, rule-governed, logical environment for analytical, left-brained individuals; and an unstructured, flexible, "discovery" environment for right-brained children. Similarly, learning environments need to be adapted to children who are shown to have specific cognitive styles and to children whose intellectual functioning is impeded by extraneous variables such as inability to concentrate, anxiety or emotional lability (Kaufman, 1979).

It is reasonably clear that real individual differences in styles of thinking and learning exist within pupils in every classroom. This is a fact of life that must be recognized by educators and teachers, so that we can provide learning environments geared toward matching the students' modes of mental functioning and at the same time provide the means to develop the other cognitive systems.

What happens inside the learner's head will determine the extent to which that person is capable of learning. The ability to learn must be viewed as the logical by-product of the number of available cognitive systems and modes of mental functioning operating inside the learner's head. For maximum learning to take place, the learner must develop a wide variety of ways to organize incoming information and evolve sufficient cognitive structures and information processing patterns for assimilating and accommodating sensory input. Learning is viewed, therefore, as the direct function of the number of cognitive systems and processes available for organizing, encoding and transforming incoming verbal-linguistic or visual-spatial input. Indeed, it could be hypothesized that learning ability should be conceptualized as a function of the number of cognitive representational systems and cognitive processes divided by the processing requirements of the task. Therefore, the following formula could be calculated to obtain a learning ability quotient.

$$\text{Learning Ability Quotient} = f \left(\frac{\text{number of cognitive systems/mental processes}}{\text{processing requirements of the task}} \right)$$

In this formula, learning disability would be defined as the discrepancy between the learner's available internal cognitive systems and mental processes and the processing demands of the educational or learning task. Consequently, when a task analysis (of reading, for example, which requires the interaction of many cognitive systems and diagnostic data) identifies the student as deficient in several cognitive representational systems but overspecialized in one mode of mental functioning, the teacher or educator can hypothesize that the student in question will, to some extent, be dysfunctional in the area of reading. By the same token, this formula would provide teachers and educators with the ability to predict possible learning disabilities as well as to develop effective remedial interventions.

Thus, if a learner has one intact cognitive system, but the task requires three mental operations, learning ability would be one divided by three, or .33. Multiplying by one hundred would give a learning quotient. Any ratio less than one hundred would signal a possible learning problem. Successful remediation would occur when the teacher alters the learning disabled child's *habits of cognition* and *modes of mental functioning* so that task demands would evoke and develop other information processing systems and contextualize the new systems to the appropriate learning environments. In this way, it would be the teacher's ability to evaluate and use the learner's unique differential modes for processing information that would bring about results and achieve learning automatically at an unconscious level.

While the above speculations may seem "far fetched", several researchers (Ingram, Mason & Blackburn, 1970; Johnson & Myklebust, 1976; Myklebust, 1965) did attempt to develop such a theory. But before we investigate this theory any further we need to discuss, in more detail, how cognitive processes affect learning.

Cognitive Processes and Learning Disabilities

Bruner's (1966) research was one of the first attempts at understanding the nature of the learner's cognitive processes and how they related to learning and thinking. He proposed that we should learn how to identify internal processing systems by correlating external behavior patterns with how a child thinks and learns.

In his pursuit of the answer to the epistemological question, "How do children know or think?" he concluded that they think in terms of cognitive sensory modalities. In other words, the child represents incoming information in terms of the visual, auditory and kinesthetic cognitive systems.

This theoretical position suggested that children could be classified according to the internal sensory modalities they employed and preferred in their thought processes. In his theoretical scheme, there were visually oriented learners who coded and organized incoming information in terms of visual images or pictures; kinesthetic learners who coded input stimulation through body sensations or internal visceral feelings; and auditory learners who engaged in verbal mediation strategies to understand instructional input. Bruner's position (1960, 1966) did not refer to learning styles so much as it referred to cognitive styles.

Figure 6

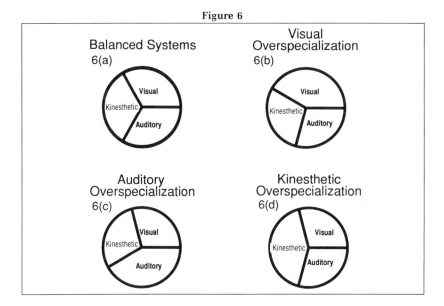

While Bruner's research began to discern behavioral patterns that seemed correlated with the preferred mode of mental functioning, he also began to suspect that children often developed strong preferences for one system over others. This preferential bias for employing one cognitive system over another created various types of learning problems (Figure 6). The child who found learning easy seemed to have developed an integrative balance between all cognitive sensory modality systems, while another learner would overspecialize in or overuse one cognitive system in all educational and instructional tasks.

We can examine this position a little further by doing the following exercise. Assume that you have a visual-cognitive representational system deficit, which simply means that you are *unable to see internal images or pictures inside your head.* No matter how hard you try to create internal images you find that all you seem to perceive is blackness! This will be hard for some of you to do because you naturally transform incoming information into clear, vivid internal visual images. However, think what it would be like without your quick access to internal pictures. For the exercise here, at least, attempt to think without images. By using this "let's pretend" framework you can gain a clearer understanding of how learning is affected by this one processing deficit. Then you may begin to understand the learning disabled child who says: "Teacher, I can't see what you are talking about or what you are saying!"

Now, answer the following questions:

1. Are you a good reader? Do you remember what you read? Do you recall the settings? Do you remember the characters and what they look like? Do you understand the overall theme of a book or a story? (Go ahead, read a story or a few pages of a book to get an idea of what this is really all about.)

2. Are you a good speller? How do you spell liaison, hypothesis or psychology? What would your spelling be like if you wrote a story?

3. How would you remember basic mathematical processes such as addition, subtraction, division, or multiplication? Would you use your fingers to count? Would you be able to solve mathematical problems?

4. What would have happened to Einstein's Theory of Relativity had he lost his ability to make internal visual images?

It is very important that you make an honest effort to do the above exercise without using internal visualization processes. Some of you probably found it difficult to avoid making internal images in response to the questions. Others of you probably wondered what all the fuss was about since you don't make pictures inside your head. Some of you probably questioned whether it was possible to make internal pictures at all!

Now, pretend that you can vividly visualize inside your head. You can create mental movies or colorful slides. And, for some panoramic scenarios, you can actually *step into the picture and feel* what it would be like to *be in that experience.* You can hear sounds, but you are unable to talk to yourself; that is, you do not use words (self-talk or self-instruction) as part of your thought processes. What subject areas might you have difficulty in learning? How would you perform in language arts? *Right now,* attempt to write a story or essay without employing internal dialogue as part of your writing strategy. What happened? Was it easy or difficult? Did you rely on your internal pictures to create the sequence of events that made up your story? Given the above internal processing system constraints, how would you respond to a phonetic approach to learning to read?

Each learner has a unique and idiosyncratic style of learning and thinking. Just like the human fingerprint, no two children are exactly alike in how they perceive, learn and think. While some children tend to develop internal cognitive system preferences (Figures 6(b), 6(c), 6(d)), others, for the most part, tend to develop a balanced interplay between all cognitive systems (Figure 6(a)).

As parents and educators, we make many false assumptions about the cognitive entry characteristics of the learner. We naturally assume that all children, to a large degree, are born with all their cognitive systems intact and fully operational. While there is a genetic predisposition to develop all cognitive sensory systems and processes, many of the systems or mental processes are elicited and evoked by interactions with the child's environment. Children learn from their parents and significant ''others'' (Do we include television?) in their environment by direct imitation or behavioral modeling of the external behavioral patterns they see in others, such as eye movements, head tilts, intonation patterns, breathing patterns and language usage. This type of direct imitation or modeling may account for the fact that some children do develop overspecialized cognitive behaviors.

A child reared in a family where music is overemphasized, and less value is placed on the visual and kinesthetic aspects of learning, may be conditioned to develop highly refined auditory learning and cognitive systems. This overemphasis on the auditory channel may predispose the child to gather information from his environment based solely on verbal-linguistic parameters and, consequently, ignore the visual and kinesthetic aspects as vital sources of information. Interestingly, the highly verbal-auditory child who does in fact ignore the visual and kinesthetic portions of his environment seems likely to have social difficulties with peers (Rourke, Fisk, & Strang, 1986). Apparently, such a child experiences difficulties because he does not attend to the nonverbal (visual and kinesthetic) aspects of interpersonal communication.

The above discussion begs the question why there is a preponderance of learning disabled children with one parent who manifests similar learning difficulties. This familial pattern has been attributed to inherited genes. But do genetics account for it all? Isn't it possible that the learning disabled child's dysfunctional learning strategies are the logical consequence of pure imitation and parental modeling? Perhaps by modeling the external behaviors of their parents, learning disabled children are unwittingly conditioned to develop similar internal cognitive processing systems and mental processes, just as children from dysfunctional families develop similar pathological behavioral patterns.

This argument can be taken one step further by a universal experience in the everyday interactions of human beings. There probably was a time in your life when you interacted with someone you really admired and respected. While you began to converse and interact with them, there came a point where you noticed that you were actually talking like them, using their gestures and even their intonation patterns. Somehow you had unconsciously modeled their external behaviors and incorporated them as part of your own ongoing behavioral repertoire. And as you engaged in acting and sounding as they did, you began to feel different on the inside. Not only did adopting their postures, gestures and words affect your internal physiological states, it also changed the way you processed information.

This may seem hard to believe, but notice the postures, breathing patterns, gestures, and eye-movement patterns that good readers use when reading a story, and compare this behavioral pattern with that often assumed by the poor reader. Once you have made a good comparative analysis of each, have the poor reader assume the posture, breathing pattern, gestures, eye-scanning patterns, head tilts and manner of holding the book, and note the difference in the reading process. In fact, I have achieved better reading rates and reading comprehension by having students hold their books at eye level or above. This did not happen in all cases, but for a large percentage of students it made a difference.

While poor readers usually slump in their chair and breathe unrhythmically, proficient readers sit up straight and breathe rhythmically and evenly. And, although they sit up in their chairs with their backs straight, they say that they feel comfortable and that they employ visual imagery to comprehend the content and the meaning of the story.

It seems plausible that learning disabled children who have cognitive representational system deficits, or who overspecialize in one cognitive system to the exclusion of others, may not be by-products of genetics so much as artifacts of environmental conditioning and parental modeling. Neurologist Dr. Andrew Sereda (1987:51) postulates, "Although these children who have difficulties with learning, compared to their schoolmates, are considered to have a spectrum of different kinds of learning problems, the author has been impressed by the fact that virtually all of these children have a superior ability to visualize mental images." Sereda (1987) goes on to explain that learning disabled children who are labelled as dyslexic are often deficient in verbal-linguistic or verbal-mediation cognitive processes. And to some extent, they cannot transfer information from one cognitive system to another.

The hypothesis that learning disabilities are the manifestation of internal cognitive system deficits or processing deficiencies provides the educator and teacher with a theoretical and practical base for designing remedial instructional learning formats. The development of new learning strategies would assist the learning disabled child to develop his other less well developed cognitive systems and teach him to apply these newly acquired cognitive ability patterns in the appropriate contexts. The teacher or educator who understands that a learner cannot visualize may be able to predict what types of learning disabilities that child is going to develop and thus provide remedial intervention to insure that these do not occur. What is needed at this point in our discussion is a means for teachers and educators to detect, identify and diagnose potential cognitive system deficits and information processing deficiencies.

Boder's Classification System

A number of investigators (Bateman, 1968; Boder, 1973, 1983; Ingram, Mason & Blackburn, 1970; Johnson & Myklebust, 1976; Myklebust, 1965) developed classifications of reading and spelling disabilities based on the underlying cognitive representational system deficit. For the most part, the subtypes of cognitive disabilities referred to deficits in the visual and auditory mental processing systems. In Boder's (1973, 1982) classification system, reading and spelling disabilities are perceived to be the direct result of an impairment in either the auditory or visual representational systems. The cognitive impairment usually represents an inability on the part of the learner to process information, either visually or auditorily. When a child is unable to code information (e.g., letters, words) visually, and is unable to recall the information by revisualizing the sequence of letters or the image of the word, he is categorized *dyseidetic.*

The dyseidetic reader/speller does not use his visual cognitive processing system to encode and store what individual letters or whole words look like. Neither can the dyseidetic reader/speller perceive letters and words as configurations or gestalts. Moreover, he has tremendous difficulty in remembering visually what the letters of the alphabet look like, and he may not be able to tell you at random what letter follows another. This deficiency in memorizing letters and whole word configurations results in a disability to learn a sight-word vocabulary. The dyseidetic learner relies primarily on an auditory cognitive system for learning to read and to spell. He learns to read phonetically, reading very slowly since he is sounding out each syllable in each word. Typical misreadings include phonetic decoding of nonphonetic words, and frequent letter and word reversals. Learning to read via a sight-word approach is next to impossible for the dyseidetic reader.

The dyseidetic speller's productions are phonetically accurate. He spells words the way they sound: for example, ''conclusion'' for ''conclusion''; ''reche'' for ''reach''; ''rizolte'' for ''result''.

In contrast, the *dysphonetic* reader or speller has great difficulty integrating sounds with their appropriate symbols. This symbol-sound deficit leads to difficulties in sounding out words, to difficulties in blending the component letters and syllables into whole word configurations, and to problems in re-auditorizing the sequence of sounds in the appropriate order. In addition, the dysphonetic reader does not develop phonetic word analysis or decoding skills; rather, he reads words globally, employing a visual spatial cognitive system to remember what the letters and words look like. The dysphonetic speller produces words that are phonetically inaccurate, relying heavily on a sight-word vocabulary and revisualization cognitive processes. The inability to sound out words or to connect the sounds with the appropriate symbols results in the dysphonetic reader frequently employing semantic substitutions (e.g., "weep" for "sob"; "funny" for "laugh"; "human" for "person"). To a large extent, the dysphonetic reader and speller relies much more on nonphonological cognitive processes.

The *alexic* or dyseidetic-dysphonetic reader/speller is deficient in both the visual and auditory cognitive systems. He has disabilities in phonetic word analysis and sight-word vocabulary, and thus tends to be a nonreader and nonspeller. During reading, the alexic child will exhibit misreadings based on wild guesses, from minimal cues such as using the first letter of a word to generate a word that looks similar. Since reading and spelling are so severely impaired, remedial efforts tend to have a poor prognosis; however, most successful remedial programs employ a third channel, the tactile-kinesthetic cognitive system, for learning letters and whole words (Bateman, 1968).

While *The Boder Test of Reading and Spelling Patterns* provides educators and teachers with diagnostic procedures for determining the type of reading and spelling patterns, the classroom teacher will need to make some modifications for it to have any practical application to the classroom. In fact, let's examine some examples in Figures 6 to 17. The results were obtained from the Wide Range Achievement Test (WRAT), and, by itself, the WRAT can provide useful information about the underlying cognitive processes responsible for reading and spelling productions. In order to understand more clearly the characteristics of each pattern, Table 3 has been developed to assist the reader in detecting and identifying Boder's reading and spelling subtypes.

It needs to be pointed out that production deficiencies outlined throughout these figures are not sufficient by themselves to measure the underlying cognitive deficits responsible for a learner's reading and spelling dysfunctions. The observer must also be sensitive to other external behavioral clues that will either confirm or invalidate the tentative diagnosis. For example, what eye movements does the learning disabled child engage in while spelling? Does the learning

TABLE 3
The Dyseidetic Reader and Speller

- has difficulty revisualizing letters and words;
- produces spelling errors in simple, frequently encountered words;
- has confusion with letters that differ in terms of spatial orientation, such as p-q, b-d, s-z;
- often reverses words; e.g., "was" for "saw"
- sounds out even simple words;
- is unable to perceive the gestalt configurations of whole words
- sounds out every word as if it hasn't been seen before, and thus cannot recognize words quickly when flashed
- has a limited sight-word recognition vocabulary
- approaches reading in an overanalytical, left hemisphere, verbal-linguistic manner;
- omits letters from words, omits words when reading, and frequently loses his place;
- spells phonetically, but usually produces phonetically accurate words;
- exhibits great difficulty in learning to spell irregular words that cannot be sounded out.

The Dysphonetic Reader and Speller
- fixates on visual-orthographic configurations of words rather than the sounds and parts;
- phonetic analysis is slow and laborious; reads syllable by syllable;
- reads globally; responds best to whole words;
- lacks phonetic skills; therefore, is unable to decipher unknown words;
- has difficulty in discriminating individual sounds within words;
- has difficulty in analyzing the sequence of sounds and syllables within words;
- has difficulty blending and integrating sounds into whole words;
- spells nonphonetically; words are based on revisualization;
- guesses at unfamiliar words, rather than applies phonetic rules.

The Alexic (Dyseidetic-Dysphonetic) Reader and Speller
- has deficiencies in both visual and auditory cognitive systems;
- spells nonphonetically, but productions are often bizarre and do not represent any known words;
- perceives neither the visual gestalt of words, nor is able to sound them out;
- slow, inconsistent and poor progress.

disabled child subvocalize or move his lips to provide you with sufficient feedback to confirm phonetic sounding-out processes? When reading, does the child decode the word through phonetic analysis or by searching visually for words that appear similar? Also, what is the learner's physiological state? What is his posture, and what is his breathing pattern? The effective educator or teacher will need to develop highly refined observation skills, especially within the classroom context.

Derek's Story

Derek is a Grade 2 student who is experiencing much difficulty in learning to read. (See Figure 7). On the WISC-R (Wechsler Intelligence Scale for Children - Revised) he achieved a verbal IQ of 106, a performance IQ of 123, and a full-scale IQ of 117 + /-5. This gave him a percentile ranking of 87 and placed him within the high average to superior range of cognitive functioning. Yet, on the Wide Range Achievement Test - Revised (WRAT-R), he received a grade equivalent of the middle of Grade 1 on the reading (word recognition) subtest, an end of Grade 1 score on the spelling subtest, and an end of Grade 1 rating on the arithmetic subtest. There is a significant discrepancy between his potential and his achievement level. This data may be interpreted by some psychodiagnosticians as indicative of a learning disability.

Further investigation, however, reveals several words spelled correctly on the WRAT-R spelling test, while the remaining words seem to be the results of wild guessing. When one looks at the type of errors produced (''boll'' for ''dress''; ''ret'' for ''reach''; ''wot'' for ''watch''; ''hit'' for ''enter''; ''goh'' for ''grown''; or ''hant'' for ''nature'') the inclination may be to classify the child as dyseidetic. His performance on the reading subtest might also appear to lend support to this tentative hypothesis. Yet, he is best classified as alexic, suggesting that he is deficient in both the visual and auditory cognitive representational systems. This was confirmed during the actual testing situation. When responding to the task demands of spelling, he frequently looked straight ahead and occasionally moved his eyes up and to the right. While he repeated a word to himself, he did not attempt to employ phonic analysis to the task at hand. He did, however, search visually for the word, but appeared to be trying to reconstruct it in bits and pieces. When he did recognize the word, he often looked up and to his left to recall the correct spelling (Flaro, 1986). On the reading subtest, he did recognize some words, but more often than not he guessed at a word, using minimal clues such as the first letter of the stimulus word. On several occasions, he just gave up and responded with, ''I don't know.''

Further questioning revealed that Derek had good metacognitive

Figure 7

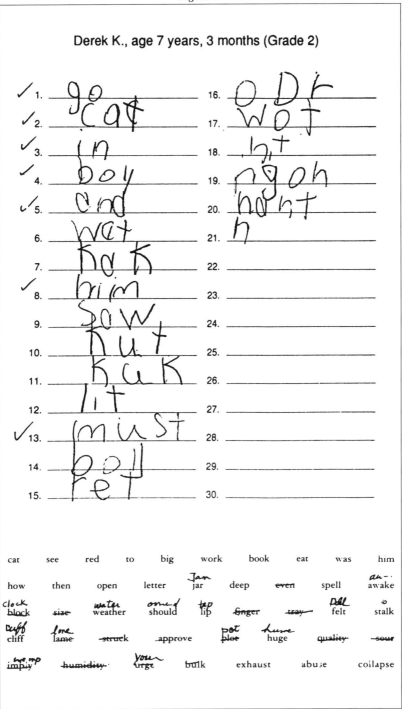

Derek K., age 7 years, 3 months (Grade 2)

awareness (awareness of his own internal cognitive systems) by ranking his preferred representational system as kinesthetic, then auditory, and then visual. This indeed seemed evident on the arithmetic subtest in which he used his fingers and subvocalizations to solve the problems. On an informal test requiring him to add 6 plus 8, he employed his fingers and subvocalizations to arrive at the answer. When asked to add 8 plus 6, he again resorted to his fingers and subvocalizations to produce the answer. This is a typical response of children who do not use internal visualization processes to see the relationships between two equations.

Derek's self-analysis on the strengths and weaknesses of his own internal cognitive systems and modes of functioning are interesting in light of his results on the WISC-R. The results on the WISC-R suggest average verbal abilities and superior nonverbal capacities. Generally, the verbal IQ can be associated with the verbal-auditory skills of the left hemisphere, while the performance IQ results are reflective of the visual-spatial abilities of the right hemisphere. This tended to be confirmed by some behavioral observations during the testing; he exhibited word finding difficulties and seemed to have expressive difficulties. He frequently found it frustrating to put his thoughts into words and often commented that he knew what it was but couldn't explain it.

These results would suggest exceptionally well-developed visual-spatial skills. On performance tests that required tactile manipulation, he performed in the superior range, but performed poorly on tasks requiring the employment of internal visualization processes. One wonders why Derek is attempting to learn to read through his weakest system, his auditory system. Is it possible that the school system's emphasis on phonics and verbal-auditory cognitive processes precluded him from further developing his visual capacities and forced him to function within his weakest cognitive system? This is certainly food for thought in light of some informal test-train-test procedures.

When Derek was asked to read simple words and then more complex ones, he did very well on the smaller units. He was unable to decode the larger, more complex words. Whenever he was asked to find smaller words within larger ones he responded very quickly. When it was pointed out to him that he could use this strategy to help him decode unfamiliar words, *and then* use phonics to sound out the rest, he reacted with surprise. Yet, further testing revealed that he could generalize this learning. Follow-up with the boy's parents indicated that he was using this cognitive strategy successfully.

The point of this case study is to show that one can use written work such as spelling quizzes to obtain a hypothesis about the nature of the learner's difficulties as well as the underlying processing styles the student is or is not using inside his head. However, *behavioral information* is also needed to substantiate the tentative hypothesis.

Derek is now in a special education resource room program where the special education teacher uses his cognitive strengths (kinesthetic and visual) as a means to improve his reading ability. She is employing visual processing strategies (external to internal) to teach him how to recognize words within words, how to recognize larger parts of words, such as 'tion', and how to apply phonetic rules as a fall-back system whenever he encounters unfamiliar words. But most important, she is using a tactile-kinesthetic approach to help Derek learn the shape of letters and words. By having him write letters on rough-textured cardboard (similar to sandpaper) and associate the sound with each letter, he is learning to recognize the external characteristics. As a final step, she traces the letters on the back of his hand and asks him to visualize each letter inside his head! Once he can connect the tactile-kinesthetic input to a visual image, she then asks him what that letter sounds like. This procedure is carried over to words, starting with smaller units and evolving into larger ones.

In four months, Derek has made substantial progress in his reading ability. His teacher has discovered that Derek does, indeed, have excellent abilities in generating internal visual images. Once Derek makes an internal image of a word and then associates it with sound, he doesn't forget it. Not only has his sight-word vocabulary increased, Derek's use of phonics has increased as well, although he prefers not to employ word analysis in decoding unfamiliar words unless his other strategies do not work.

Derek's parents are amazed at the progress he has made over the four-month period. They say that he now brings books home to read and really seems to enjoy this activity. He is even beginning to write his own stories. Derek's parents have also noticed that he seems to be a much happier child.

Anita's Story

While Derek's reading and spelling deficits are representative of the alexic pattern, his difficulties are considered mild when compared to those of Anita, whose work is shown in Figure 8. Anita is a Grade 2 student, aged 7 years and 7 months, who is experiencing severe problems in learning to read. While she possesses average intellectual capabilities, her achievement level is well below her potential. Resource room testing placed her reading at the pre-primer level.

Results of her spelling and reading subtest productions indicate an alexic pattern of reading and spelling dysfunctions. Her spellings are typical of an alexic speller, with one or two words spelled correctly and others badly misspelled. There is some evidence to suggest that Anita occasionally attempts to use phonics to spell some words (eg.,

Figure 8

Anita, Grade 2, aged 7 years, 7 months

1. Go
2. caTe (cat)
3. ne (in)
4. boe (boy)
5. ode (and)
6. Wel (Will)
7. mogve (make)
8. hme (him)
9. Sa (say)
10. aTe (cut)
11. ceTe (Cook)
12. laTe (light)
13. maTe (must)
14. Gose (dress)
15. eTa (reach)

16. ode (order)
17. oaTe (Watch)
18. nTre (enter)
19. gene (grown)
20. noie (nature)
21.
22.
23.
24.
25.
26.
27.
28.
29.
30.

cat	see	red	to	big	work	book	eat	was	him
how	then	open	letter	jar	deep	even	spell	awake
block	size	weather	should	lip	finger	tray	felt	stalk
cliff	lame	struck	approve	plot	huge	quality	sour

"boe" for "boy"; "hme" for "him"; "ntre" for "enter"). Yet, on looking over her recognition word scores, there is no evidence whatsoever that she employed phonetic word analysis. Like most typical alexic patterns, she generates words based on wild guesses or uses minimal cues to produce other words that might look somewhat like the stimulus word.

Behavioral observations revealed that, when spelling, Anita frequently looked down and to the right, and occasionally down and to the left. There were no indications of internal dialogue. Further investigation of Anita's metacognitive awareness suggested that she made no internal images, seldom talked to herself except to scold herself, and experienced mostly feelings. Given her hierarchy of cognitive representational systems, you can understand how frustrating school learning must be for her.

While she has been in a special education resource room for over six months, progress seems slow and tedious. Anita does not respond to visual and auditory processes, seeming to prefer the tactile-kinesthetic approach to reading and spelling. By all accounts, her prognosis is poor, and special placement may need to be considered.

Mary's Story

Mary's results on the WRAT (Figure 9) suggest that she primarily employs visual-internal cognitive processes to spell and read. Whenever Mary is unable to revisualize a word, she uses her auditory-phonic skills to sound it out. While most of these attempts are phonetically accurate, because she is unable to use a visual criterion (how it looks) to determine a word's correctness, she is forced to rely solely on using how a word sounds as the means to spell or to recognize it. While Mary has access to both systems, her auditory system seems to be less well developed than her visual, suggesting a proclivity toward some later form of dysphonetic difficulties. At present, however, she is doing reasonably well in Grade 3.

Mark's Story

For another illustration of Boder's subtypes of spelling and reading dysfunctions, let us look now at Mark and his results on the WRAT (Figure 10). Mark, a Grade 2 student, aged 7 years and 8 months, is having difficulty learning. His teacher has recognized that he is overly active in class, cannot sit still, and is always up and on the go. He wanders around the classroom, talks to his neighbors, and seems unable to control himself. A teacher's questionnaire on hyperactivity and the Personality Inventory for Children (PIC) confirm the presence of hyperactivity.

During the testing period, Mark exhibited overactive, restless and fidgety behavior. He was easily distracted by extraneous stimuli and

Figure 9

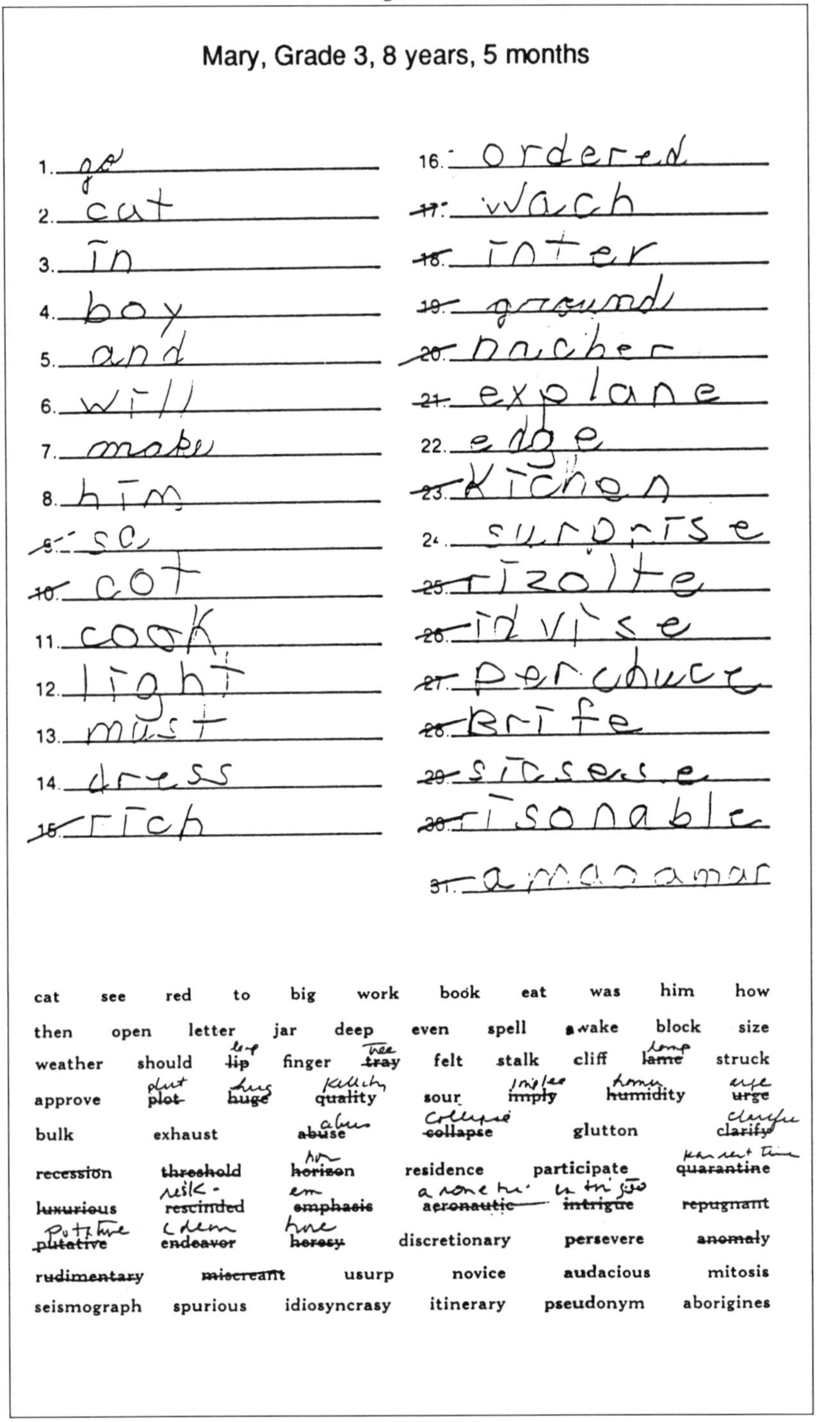

Mary, Grade 3, 8 years, 5 months

1. go
2. cat
3. in
4. boy
5. and
6. will
7. make
8. him
9. se
10. cot
11. cook
12. light
13. must
14. dress
15. rich

16. ordered
17. wach
18. inter
19. ground
20. nucher
21. explane
22. edge
23. kichen
24. suronise
25. rizolte
26. idvise
27. perchuce
28. brife
29. sicsene
30. risonable
31. a mananar

cat	see	red	to	big	work	book	eat	was	him	how
then	open	letter	jar	deep	even	spell	awake	block	size	
weather	should	lip	finger	tray	felt	stalk	cliff	lame	struck	
approve	plot	huge	quality	sour	imply	humidity	urge			
bulk	exhaust	abuse	collapse			glutton	clarify			
recession	threshold	horizon	residence	participate	quarantine					
luxurious	rescinded	emphasis	aeronautic	intrigue	repugnant					
plutative	endeavor	heresy	discretionary	persevere	anomaly					
rudimentary	miscreant	usurp	novice	audacious	mitosis					
seismograph	spurious	idiosyncrasy	itinerary	pseudonym	aborigines					

Figure 10

Mark, Grade 2, aged 7 years, 8 months

had quite a difficult time staying with a task. He was rather verbal and often went off at inconsequential tangents. When asked to explain what he did inside his head, he responded by saying he mostly made pictures, had feelings that were often associated with the pictures, and seldom, if ever, talked to himself. Lack of verbal mediation processes seemed to contribute substantially to his hyperactivity, since, if he saw something externally or internally, he would react to it without thinking. Here, thinking must be defined as the deployment of internal auditory processes: internal dialogue/inner speech.

When asked to spell words, Mark responded by looking up and to the right, then down and to the right, and frequently laterally to the right. On many occasions, the basic patterns were there but arranged differently. He seemed to lack consistent eye movements when spelling, but was predominantly a right-eye mover. This meant that in response to input instruction, his initial eye-movement was to the right. In fact, 90 percent of Mark's eye movement patterns seemed to be lateralized to the right side.

As can be seen, most of Mark's spellings were based on a visual approach to coding words. He could revisualize what they looked like, but if they were not in his visual lexicon he resorted to guessing rather than sounding them out. His phonics were poorly developed, confirming his statement that he seldom talked to himself. Similar findings occurred on the reading subtest where he exhibited good sight-word recognition but guessed at words he did not instantly recognize. This impulsive pattern is also characteristic of children who predominantly use right-brain processes or a simultaneous style of processing. They attempt to learn by storing the whole word based on its configurational and gestalt attributes and then recalling the word by revisualizing an image of the whole nonphonological unit.

It was decided to attack Mark's weakest area by introducing the THINK ALOUD program, which is aimed at developing internal mediation strategies and self-instructional processes. The problem-solving steps and self-instructional tasks were systematically linked with the appropriate eye-movement patterns so that we could build in automaticity. This meant that whenever Mark verbalized (externally) the procedural self-instructional steps, or asked himself the appropriate question, he would look down to the left and pair this eye-movement pattern with his external vocalizations. This form of classical conditioning was designed to build into the brain an automatic pattern associated with self-talk. By using this pattern, we would have a way to test the effectiveness of the training program, because if it worked we should see an automatic downward left-eye movement whenever he began to talk to himself. Then, once this program was behaviorally established, we could generalize to other contexts: spelling, reading, hyperactive behaviors.

The final step in this procedure was to teach Mark to internalize the strategy. To do this, he would look down to his left, say the instructions aloud, and then whisper them to himself and, finally, repeat the self-instructional steps inside his head. Later on, we could test for the behavioral automaticity of the training strategy.

Follow-up training of about three months revealed good progress. Not only was Mark's hyperactive behavior reduced considerably, his response to learning phonics was also much improved. Further follow-up will need to be done in order to evaluate the effectiveness of this training procedure. At present, it looks very promising.

Chad's Story

As a final example of Boder's subtypes of spelling and reading patterns, we will examine the spelling and reading performances of Chad on the WRAT, level 11 (Figure 11). Chad is a Grade 8 student, aged 15 years, 7 months, who has always had great difficulty with learning in school. He was placed in a junior (vocational) opportunity classroom where he is doing reasonably well. As can be seen from his spelling results, he uses primarily a phonetic approach to decoding words. In fact, the correctly spelled words have been learned through continuous auditory rehearsal. At night, his parents would work with him, having him repeat each word until it was spelled correctly. This constant hear-say practice has undoubtedly given him the means to become a fair speller. His characteristic spelling productions suggest a dyseidetic deficiency. While he appears to learn words phonetically, he does in fact have to sound out each word again in order to spell it. On the reading test, he recognized quite a few words but, more often than not, he resorted to phonetic word analysis decoding skills. Even with words he seemed to recognize, he first sounded them out to make sure that what he said would be correct.

Chad does not form any internal imagery. He says that when he tries to generate internal images or pictures all he perceives is blackness. In fact, he doesn't respond to after-images, possibly indicating some form of neurological damage. Further investigation on the part of the examiner revealed that Chad had suffered some brain damage at birth which resulted in lateralization to the right hemisphere. Recent neuropsychological testing substantiates this hypothesis. However, Chad's left hemisphere is fully operational, so that he can learn to read and spell through verbal-auditory methods. His profile is typical of dyseidetic children who do not exhibit any evidence of neurological damage.

Figure 11

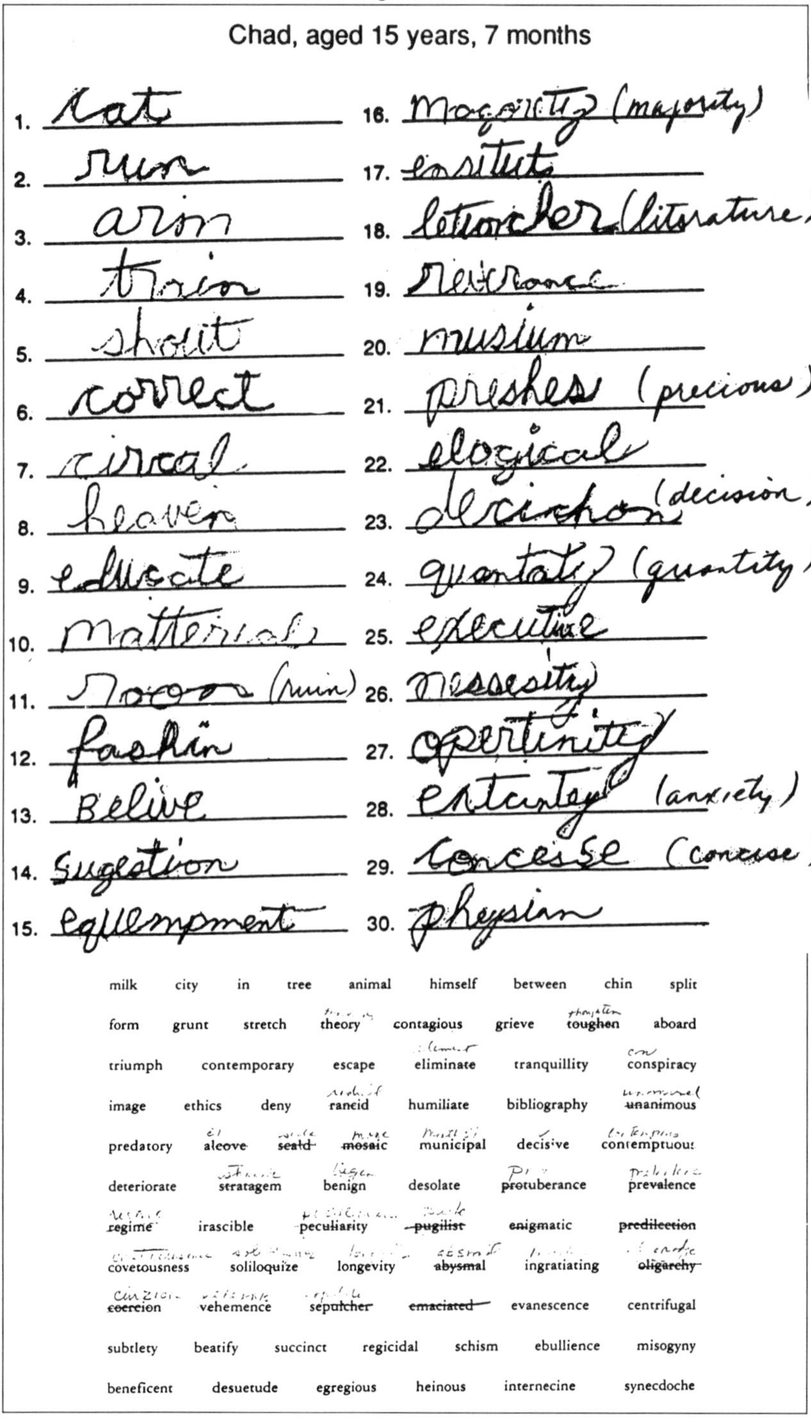

Chad, aged 15 years, 7 months

1. _Cat_
2. _run_
3. _arm_
4. _train_
5. _shout_
6. _correct_
7. _circal_
8. _heaven_
9. _educate_
10. _mattrials_
11. _noon_ (noon)
12. _fashin_
13. _Belive_
14. _Sugestion_
15. _eqllempment_
16. _majoritz_ (majority)
17. _ensitute_
18. _letrocher_ (literature)
19. _Nertranc_
20. _musium_
21. _preshes_ (precious)
22. _elogical_
23. _decichon_ (decision)
24. _quantaly_ (quantity)
25. _executine_
26. _nessesity_
27. _opertinity_
28. _entertey_ (anxiety)
29. _conceise_ (concise)
30. _pheysim_

milk	city	in	tree	animal	himself	between	chin	split
form	grunt	stretch	theory	contagious	grieve	toughen	aboard	
triumph	contemporary	escape	eliminate	tranquillity	conspiracy			
image	ethics	deny	rancid	humiliate	bibliography	unanimous		
predatory	aleove	seald	mosaic	municipal	decisive	contemptuous		
deteriorate	stratagem	benign	desolate	protuberance	prevalence			
regime	irascible	peculiarity	pugilist	enigmatic	predilection			
covetousness	soliloquize	longevity	abysmal	ingratiating	oligarchy			
coercion	vehemence	sepulcher	emaciated	evanescence	centrifugal			
subtlety	beatify	succinct	regicidal	schism	ebullience	misogyny		
beneficent	desuetude	egregious	heinous	internecine	synecdoche			

While Boder's classification system of reading and spelling dysfunctions emphasises internal deficiencies in an individual's cognitive systems and processing styles, it does not paint the whole picture. Its emphasis on cognitive styles to the exclusion of learning styles is somewhat misleading. Learning is a function of the number of cognitive systems an individual has for organizing incoming information or instruction. While the sensory input channels (vision, audition, kinesthesis) are extremely important for learning to take place—and our learning style preferences/biases predispose us to pay selective attention to certain aspects of our environment—it is the number of cognitive systems and processing styles available for coding, organizing and transforming incoming stimulation that determines the extent and level of our learning.

A number of investigators (Johnson and Myklebust, 1967; Killen, 1975, 1978; Myklebust, Bannochie and Killen, 1971) have postulated that learning is a by-product of the interrelations among input channels, cognitive systems and output responses. The primary learning systems of audition, vision and tactile-kinesthesia provide peripheral information which is transferred into the cognitive systems and mental processes of the central nervous system. Input stimulation received through audition is processed in the temporal lobe, while visual data is processed in the occipital lobe, and tactile-kinesthetic sensation is organized and interpreted in the parietal lobes (Killen, 1975). This proposal suggests that neurological processes are sensory specific, implying that the cognitive systems are associated with sensory modalities that process input information, translating the cognitive information into output behavioral responses. The information received through the learning senses is transferred to the cognitive perceptual modality systems and then coded or organized into neurosensory or modality systems; that is, the input data is translated into internal pictures, sounds, internal self-talk or internal feelings.

While an auditory stimulus (e.g., a word) may be translated into a visual representation, the information must be organized into neurosensory or modality systems translatable into all other cognitive systems so that the input data can be matched to other stored knowledge. Mismatching triggers off accommodative cognitive processes located in each cerebral hemisphere: sequential, simultaneous and integrative cognitive styles. When one input sensory system is converted into only one cognitive modality, this creates cognitive inflexibility and produces behavioral responses characteristic of functional fixedness. This was demonstrated in the discussion of the Boder (1983) classification system of reading and spelling dysfunctional patterns. The learning disabled child would hear a word to be spelled and translate that input stimulus into an

Figure 12

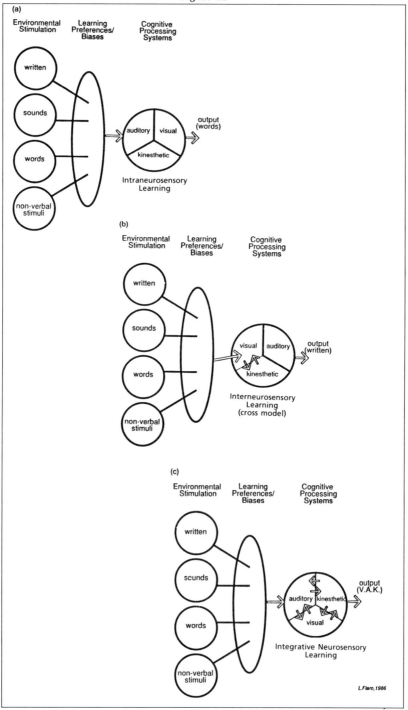

auditory cognitive system. He would then use this system to operate on the input stimulus by either employing word analysis skills or other verbal-mediation cognitive processes.

This internal processing system did not convert the information into the other cognitive systems to determine the correctness of the final output response. Instead, the learning disabled learner would write the word without paying attention to the visual features or whether the word looked right or not. Indeed, the learning disabled learner used solely an auditory-internal criterion—how it sounded—rather than combining the visual-cognitive processes to evaluate the final outcome.

When information is received through one learning system and then transduced into only one cognitive modality system, wherein this data is not translated into the language of the other cognitive complexes, this type of representation is called *intraneurosensory learning* (Figure 12 (a)). This is best represented by having the student repeat a series of words or sounds that are received orally. The words or sounds received through the input channels are mediated by an internal auditory cognitive system, such as inner language, and then transformed into an appropriate output (verbal/nonverbal) response. Thus, one modality is activated and involved with reception, processing and expression.

Interneurosensory learning occurs when input data is processed initially in one cognitive modality system and then is transduced into a different representational system prior to an output response (Figure 12 (b)). As an example of this type of learning, consider the child who hears a verbal (auditory) instruction, translates this into cognitive imagery (visual) and then verbalizes a comment about the instruction. Now, while intrasensory learning precludes the learner from transforming cognitive information into another modality system, interneurosensory learning provides the learner with the means for translating information into one other system. In intraneurosensory learning, the boundaries separating the cognitive systems appear to be impermeable to each other, which is neurologically analogous to intercerebral disconnection whereby two parts of the brain have lost their ability to communicate with each other; while interneurosensory learning represents intercommunication between two cognitive modality systems, but not the other sensory structures. This type of learning represents cross-modal processing; for example, when listening to classical music and responding emotionally to it, the music is transformed into visual images of a time and a place that best characterizes that feeling. Our language is replete with phrases that typify this cross-modal processing: "colorful music"; "emotionally charged words"; "pleasant sounds". Another example of this type of learning occurs when the student is asked to spell a word. Upon hearing the word, he immediately begins to sound it out; this is subsequently translated into visual constructions of syllabic parts, which are then written on paper.

The ability to employ all cognitive modalities simultaneously so that all systems are brought to bear upon the input information is called *integrative neurosensory learning* (Figure 12 (c)). Integrative neurosensory learning is extremely important for extracting meaning from written words, as well as understanding the content of a story. Whenever you read a novel and become so deeply engrossed in the story that you feel what the characters feel, see the setting, and hear the voices and environmental sounds, you have literally stepped into the experience and simultaneously orchestrated all sensory-modality systems. This networking of all cognitive systems is probably a prerequisite for cognitive flexibility and the development of higher level cognitive thinking abilities.

Some Procedural Steps for Working With Learning Disabled Children

This chapter has stressed the importance of knowing what cognitive systems (visual, auditory, kinesthetic) and mental mediating processes (sequential, simultaneous, integrative) are available to the learner for the purpose of encoding, organizing and transducing instructional input. It has dealt with various types of learning (intraneurosensory, interneurosensory, integrative neurosensory) based on the concepts of intracommunication, intercommunication and interconnection between all cognitive representational systems, as well as the vitally important ability to translate information from one cognitive modality into another cognitive system.

As well, several examples of dysfunctional spelling and reading patterns were presented to provide the teacher or educator with an initial basis for delineating the learning disabled child's underlying cognitive systems and mental mediating processing deficits that contributed significantly to the observed production deficiencies. In this way, the teacher and the educator could begin to understand the importance of diagnosing the types of systems impaired, the number of systems impaired, and the degree of impairment, in all cognitive systems. Similarly, the analysis of each reading and spelling pattern was designed to show the teacher and educator how important information about a learner's habits of cognition or learning strategies can be obtained from examples of classroom work or standardized test results.

In most cases today, the identification of learning disabilities is based on test instruments purported to measure precisely the underlying cognitive processing systems. Further examination, however, reveals that most test instruments measure a child's ability according to statistical results, and use this validation as the hallmark for concluding the presence or the absence of a learning dysfunction rather than as a means for understanding the *learner's processing differences*. While this testing method can be useful in and of itself, many tests and structured remedial programs are designed to make the learning disabled child fit the researcher's theoretical position. Each professional group (psychologists, neurologists, opthamologists, psycholinguists, speech pathologists and special educators) will present a different theory on the causes, diagnoses and treatment of learning disabilities. With all the theories, diagnostic criteria, treatment procedures and remedial programs that are being vehemently advocated by different professional groups, paradoxically the number of children who are failing in the educational arena has not decreased.

What has been stressed throughout this book is that as educators, teachers and professionals we need to learn to appreciate the processing capabilities of each child. In the case of learning disabilities, we need to learn more about the cognitive systems and mental mediating processes that account for learning differences in the learning disabled child. We need to discover what cognitive deficiencies are contributory factors to the incidence of learning disabilities. We also need to understand what cognitive variables make it possible for some children to learn, while others struggle in a system that offers few answers. The following questions/steps are offered as guidelines for gathering appropriate diagnostic information about the learning disabled child. These questions need to be answered by the educator before remedial hypotheses and treatment procedures are begun.

1. What is the specific learning disability of this child?
2. What can the student presently do well?
3. What can't the learning disabled student presently do?
4. What is his (or her) current level of academic functioning in strong and weak subject areas?
5. What cognitive systems and mental processes are needed in order to do well on the dysfunctional task?
6. Does this child favor one cognitive system over the others?
7. Does he overspecialize in one system without employing the resources and capabilities of the other cognitive systems?
8. What are the eye-movement patterns associated with poor performance on a particular task (task analysis)?
9. Is this student a left-eye mover or a right-eye mover? Does he spend more time accessing information by looking up, gazing laterally, or shifting his eyes downward?

10. Can he translate information from one cognitive representational modality into another cognitive system?
11. What spelling and reading patterns does this student exhibit on informal tests? On formal tests?
12. What, specifically, does the teacher or parent want him to do in terms of performance?
13. What exactly are the processing requirements of the task or the subject area with which he is having the learning difficulty?
14. What, specifically, is the student aware of doing inside his head (metacognition)?
15. What words does the student use to discuss his internal cognitive strategies for performing a cognitive task?
16. What is the difference in physiology between those academic tasks he can do and those subject areas in which he has learning dysfunctions?

These questions should be kept in mind while you are gathering information about a student's current level of academic functioning. Initial assessment data should be obtained from formal and informal tests, teacher perceptions, classroom observations and behavioral information. By behavioral information, it is intended that the examiner in question test the child's deficiencies to determine if consistent behavioral responses are evident and contributory to the present problem. This takes the form of asking children to produce output responses that represent their problem area, so that you can gather important information about how that student processes instructions.

In the classroom, you have observed that one student is having tremendous difficulty with spelling tests, as well as showing poor spelling on writing assignments. The results of formal (standardized) tests indicate that he is two years or more below his present grade level. You know from previous intellectual and cognitive evaluations that he is above average. During spelling tests, you notice that he responds to your verbal instructions by looking up, right, and then down, right. This behavioral strategy is consistent the majority of times. Similarly, examination of his spelling productions shows a dyseidetic pattern. Further investigation reveals abdominal breathing patterns, a slouched posture and a continuous "looking down" strategy.

The next step requires you to ask the student direct questions about his awareness of the internal cognitive processes he employs to spell words. What cognitive systems does he use to translate your verbal instructions into motor responses? Can he translate information coded in one system into other mental systems? This information can be obtained by having the child spell orally for you in an environment that is safe and secure for the child to perform. As you ask him to spell a word, notice changes in physiology, posture, head tilts and eye movements. Have him repeat several oral productions, noting if there is a regularity of behavioral patterns for spelling. This constitutes a *strategy* he is using to produce the words. Once you have detected this behavioral pattern, have him spell another word, and ask him what he did inside his head. Did he say the word to himself and try to sound it out? Did he try to picture it? Or did he just feel that he couldn't do it? Ask him to rank order these systems from most used to least used.

You then need to determine which systems are functional. Even though he may rank them as visual, auditory and kinesthetic, and indicate that his kinesthetic system is least developed, this does not mean he cannot employ this sensory modality. In addition, you need to know if he can translate information from one representational system into another cognitive modality. You can ask him to listen to a word and try to get a picture of it; this suggests auditory to visual translation. You can ask him to listen to your verbal request, repeat it to himself, and then attempt to sound it out; this represents external-auditory to internal-auditory to verbal-auditory. As he sounds out the word, can he translate these phonemic equivalents into visual representations? This constitutes an internal translation of auditory information into the visual system. This procedure is designed to teach you how to gather important information through verbal questioning and behavioral observations in order to determine the type of learning systems that are operational and those that are not.

Once you have gathered sufficient information about the nature of the child's difficulty, you then go to the next step: the generation of potential hypotheses. Given the information you have gathered in the previous steps, you should be able to develop some intervention strategies that may correct the learning difficulty. This means that you provide the student with a test-train-test format in which you teach him a new procedure or learning format for becoming a good speller. The procedure could be to have him look at a word, see it with his mind's eye, and then spell it for you. Using this procedure, you'll find that he isn't making internal pictures, but, rather, he is still trying to sound out the word. To overcome this automatic program, ask him to pretend that his mind is a camera. The camera can take snapshots of what it sees, but, in the case of spelling words, he isn't allowed to say them to himself, nor is he permitted to sound them out. At this point, depending on your skill, you may ask him to look up and left to remember the visual image of the word. As a result of this remedial procedure, you will find that he can see the word in his mind and spell it. In fact, he can even spell it backwards! Your ongoing behavioral and verbal feedback suggest that this procedure will work for him. The final step is to have him contextualize it to his classroom. The ability to generalize this new learning to other learning environments, as resource room teachers will attest, is most important. You, the teacher, must provide positive feedback that will direct him to employ the cognitive format that he has learned with you. This may take the form of *gently* reminding him to look up and see the word, and then to copy it down on paper for you.

A successful evaluation of a new learning and cognitive strategy should be based on the following criteria: (1) Behavioral patterning; Does the individual exhibit different behavioral responses from the original request? In other words, is his present external behavior different from what was assessed initially? (2) Automaticity: Does the individual perform the new strategy with as much or more automaticity than the old cognitive strategy? If he still uses his old strategy, the new learning format has not been installed adequately. (3) Has he generalized his new cognitive learnings and systems to other areas of learning? (4) Does his performance on spelling tests change as a result of the newly acquired strategy? Those procedures and discussions will be elaborated upon in Chapter 4.

What needs to be pointed out here is that the proposed set of guidelines requires well-developed sensory acuity and observation skills on the part of the teacher and educator. The same procedures can be applied effectively by parents who, in fact, can do much in the way of automatizing the cognitive and learning formats. Parents are a vital source of assistance and should be involved in the treatment program.

Suggested Exercises for Parents and Teachers

Exercise one: Representational System Preference Inventory

Rank order each of the following statements with the numbers 1 to 4, placing the number 1 beside the phrase that best describes you, number 2 beside the phrase that next best describes you, and so on. Do that for each of the twelve statements. Scoring information follows the test.

1. I am more likely to say:
- ☐ important decisions are matters of feeling
- ☐ important decisions are ones I tune in to
- ☐ important decisions show my point of view
- ☐ important decisions are logical and thoughtful

2. I am most likely to be influenced by someone:
- ☐ with a nicely modulated voice
- ☐ who looks attractive
- ☐ who says sensible things
- ☐ who gives me a good feeling

3. If I want to know how someone is:
- ☐ I observe their appearance
- ☐ I check how they are feeling
- ☐ I listen to their tone of voice
- ☐ I attend to what they are saying

4. I prefer to:
- ☐ modulate the volume and tuning on a stereo system
- ☐ consider the most intellectually relevant points concerning an interesting subject
- ☐ choose superbly comfortable furniture
- ☐ find rich color combinations

5. I am effective at making sense of new facts and data:
- ☐ my ear is very attuned to the sounds in my surroundings
- ☐ I feel very sensitive to the clothing that touches my body
- ☐ I picture bright colors when I look at a room

6. If people want to know how I am:
- ☐ they should know about my feelings
- ☐ they should look at what I am wearing
- ☐ they should listen to what I say
- ☐ they should hear the intonations in my voice

7. I am more likely to:
- ☐ hear what facts you know
- ☐ see the pictures you paint
- ☐ empathize with your feelings
- ☐ tune in to your harmonious message

8. I find something more believable if:
- [ ] I can see it
- [ ] I hear about it
- [ ] I feel it is real
- [ ] I hear how it is said

9. Where my family is concerned:
- [ ] I usually have a strong sense about their well-being
- [ ] I can picture their faces, clothes and small, visible details
- [ ] I know the way they think about most issues, especially their significant ideas about things
- [ ] When I hear the voice intonations and inflections of any member of my immediate family I can instantly identify the speaker

10. I prefer to:
- [ ] learn new concepts
- [ ] learn to do new things
- [ ] learn to hear new things
- [ ] learn to see new possibilities

11. When I think about decisions, I will probably:
- [ ] conclude that important decisions are a matter of feeling
- [ ] decide that important decisions are the ones I tune in to
- [ ] decide that important decisions are the ones I see clearest
- [ ] decide that important decisions are logical and thoughtful

12. I can remember:
- [ ] how a friend sounds
- [ ] what a friend looks like
- [ ] the things a friend says to me
- [ ] how I feel about a friend

Scoring
Step 1: Copy the answers from the test on to the lines below.

1.
- [ ] K (Kinesthetic)
- [ ] A (Auditory)
- [ ] V (Visual)
- [ ] D (Digital)

2.
- [ ] A
- [ ] V
- [ ] D
- [ ] K

3.
- [ ] V
- [ ] K
- [ ] A
- [ ] D

4.
- [ ] A
- [ ] D
- [ ] K
- [ ] V

5.
- [ ] D
- [ ] A
- [ ] K
- [ ] V

6.
- [ ] K
- [ ] V
- [ ] D
- [ ] A

7. ☐ D
    ☐ V
    ☐ K
    ☐ A

8. ☐ V
    ☐ D
    ☐ K
    ☐ A

9. ☐ K
    ☐ V
    ☐ D
    ☐ A

10. ☐ D
    ☐ K
    ☐ A
    ☐ V

11. ☐ K
    ☐ A
    ☐ V
    ☐ D

12. ☐ A
    ☐ V
    ☐ D
    ☐ K

Step 2: Add the numbers associated with each letter. There will be a possible twelve entries for each letter. Use the following table to record the entries and to add up the totals for each letter.

Scoring Chart

	V	K	A	D
1				
2				
3				
4				
5				
6				
7				
8				
9				
10				
11				
12				

Step 3. A comparison of the total scores in columns V, K, A and D will give you some information about your relative preferences (hierarchy) for each of the representational systems.

The first exercise was designed to give you, the reader, some information about learning styles, representational systems/cognitive styles and hemispheric styles. While the inventories were intended to give you some insight into how you think, process and organize information in various contexts, they do not represent definitive or categorical answers. Describing a student as visual, auditory, kinesthetic, sequential, simultaneous, left-brained, right-brained or integrated, provides you with valuable information about how that individual learns, but at the same time it's no different than labelling him learning disabled. Each child is unique in how he or she handles information and the demands of an academic environment. It is important, therefore, to be able to gather as much information as possible about a student before identifying his or her learning strategies. Similarly, remedial plans and programs should be based on a myriad of factors. The following exercises are designed to teach you specific sensory-acuity skills by observing external behavioral patterns and correlating them with internal information-processing strategies. Such external behaviors as eye movements, head tilts and words seem to "go along" with internal cognitive processes. As a teacher working with learning disabled students, it will be very important to use the information you have gathered.

Exercise Two:
Each day, begin to listen to the words students use to answer questions or to explain concepts. This will provide you with information about the type of cognitive system a student employs as part of his or her thinking processes. It may be wise to write down sensory-specific words the student(s) use(s) during discussions. Does the student use visual words, such as see, clear, focus, visualize, imagine, picture, describe? Auditory words, such as hear, say, clicks, say to myself, discuss, sounds like? Kinesthetic words, such as feel, in touch, grasp, get a handle on, struggle, stuck or depressed? Does the individual student use unspecified, digital words, such as know, think, understand, aware, believe, compute, calculate? Does the student use sequential words, including following, one step at a time, next, come after, come next, going after, successively, one thing after another, on the one hand, stepping stones, afterwards, piecemeal, part by part, in bits and pieces? Or does he express himself by using simultaneous words, such as all at once, in the same breath, immediate, wholly, entirely, grand view, bird's eye view, one and all, every inch? What gestures might go along with sequential and simultaneous processing words? Do the short test below and determine whether the statements are visual (V), auditory (A), kinesthetic (K), sequential (SQ), or simultaneous (SM).
1. ☐ I don't see what you are talking about.
2. ☐ Teacher, this doesn't feel right.
3. ☐ Can you repeat that. I didn't hear it.
4. ☐ Well, as I read, I get the whole idea--what the story is telling me.
5. ☐ Teacher, I just can't get a handle on what you are talking about.

6. ☐ My dad always listens to what I say to him. He talks to me about any subject.
7. ☐ My mom and I don't see eye to eye. She just doesn't see the world the way I see it.
8. ☐ When I yell at a child, I feel so guilty I just want to scream at myself for being such an idiot.
9. ☐ You know, this stuff smells pretty fishy to me. It really leaves a bad taste in my mouth.
10. ☐ When I approach a problem, I have to gather each and every fact before I can piece together all the information and find the right solution.

Exercise Three:

Kinsbourne (1972), and Lefevre, Starck and Lambert (1977), observed that when an individual is thinking about verbal material his eyes will move up and to the right. When the same person is thinking about spatial information, his eyes will move up and to the left. In normally organized right-handers, language abilities are lateralized to the left hemisphere, whereas visual-spatial capacities are located in the right hemisphere. Thus, left-eye movements activate right hemispheric cortical activity, and right-eye movements elicit left cortical activity. This occurs because each cerebral hemisphere has a built-in (innate) attention bias that orients (gaze, head tilts, body turning, gestures) toward the opposite (contralateral) side of the body. For example, take the cardboard cylinder from a roll of paper towel or something similar, or fashion a piece of paper into a tube. Now, imagining the cylinder to be a telescope, raise it to your eye and peer through it. Whichever eye you press against the telescope will be your dominant eye, and the contralateral hemisphere produced the orientation. Similarly, give a round of applause for an imaginary stage performance. Did you clap your right hand into your left hand? Or the left hand into your right hand? The difference has to do with hemispheric attentional bias, as well as other factors.

As teachers and parents, begin to pay attention to how children move their eyes in response to questions (use Figure 5). When you ask a child to spell a word, where does he move his eyes? When asked to add some numbers, where does he move his eyes? If you ask a student to give a word definition, what eye movement do you perceive? Once you have begun to notice eye-movement patterns, take the time to ask the child what he is doing inside his head. While introspectionism and self-reporting have been dismissed as unscientific, Mischel (1981) has concluded that children have excellent metacognitive awareness about their internal cognitive processes. You may be pleasantly surprised at the number of things children can tell you about their internal processing strategies and how they use them in their thought processes. Some adults have a similar cognitive awareness about their thought processes. Einstein, for example, stated that he never used language (words) or internal dialogue as part of his thinking style. Rather, he employed visual imagery and internal kinesthetic and tactile sensations (Williams, 1983).

CHAPTER 4

CONQUERING SPELLING AND CREATIVE WRITING LEARNING DISABILITIES THROUGH COGNITIVE ABILITY PATTERNING

IN THE FIRST THREE chapters, we repeatedly stressed the importance of being able to detect and to identify underlying cognitive structures and mental operations in order to overcome learning disabilities. The model presented in Chapter 2 and expounded on in Chapter 3, hypothesized that deficits in learning ability are the logical by-product of a deficiency in the number of cognitive systems a student needs to code, organize, transform and transduce incoming instructional information. Whenever the number of cognitive systems is equal to or greater than the processing requirements of a given task, the student will be able to learn. Conversely, when task demands are greater than the student's available number of cognitive systems, a learning disability will likely arise. The ability to transfer information within and between cognitive systems is a requisite process for learning. In many learning disabled children, this ability is severely lacking, especially in the type of learning referred to as integrative neurosensory. Children with this learning deficit cannot function simultaneously in two cognitive systems.

It was also hypothesized that many learning disabled children seem to become overspecialized in one cognitive system, to the exclusion of the other mental processes. Similarly, they are likely to form a preference for using a particular hemispheric style: sequential or simultaneous. Hemispheric bias predisposes them to develop specific cognitive systems, such as the visual-spatial, and underdevelop other mental modes such as verbal-linguistic. Overuse of one hemispheric style and the attendant cognitive system(s) produces one-sided cerebral functioning. The lack of use, or "cerebral atrophy", predisposes the learning disabled child to approach all learning tasks by applying the same cognitive systems and hemispheric styles in a rigid, inflexible manner. The learned cognitive bias is overgeneralized to all learning environments and, in many cases, inappropriately brought to bear upon learning tasks that require the use of other information processing systems. In addition, the bias for overspecialization naturally prevents the learning disabled child from developing integrative neurosensory learning; a necessary condition for higher cognitive functions such as conceptualization and inferential reasoning.

Finally, it was proposed that all cognitive processes and preferred hemispheric styles are intimately associated with external behavior patterns. That is, the learning disabled child's cognitive abilities, information processing systems and mental modes of functioning can be detected and identified on the basis of external behaviors exhibited while he or she is performing a particular cognitive task. A preference for left-hemispheric processing and its attendant emphasis on verbal-linguistic abilities will produce a right-body or behavioral orientation. A predisposition for employing the cognitive-visual-spatial processes of the right hemisphere will create an attentional bias for orienting to the left side (Kinsbourne, 1972). This hemispheric attentional bias will produce contralateral behavioral responses in the learning disabled child which can be detected through observation of head tilts, eye movements and hand gestures. The need to behaviorally orient oneself to one side or the other to activate the contralateral hemisphere and its accompanying cognitive processes may create problems for students who are sitting on the wrong side of the classroom (Gur, Gur and Marshalek, 1975: Kane, 1979; Morton and Kershner, 1987; Schroeder, 1976). Indeed, the research of Morton and Kershner (1987: 106) concluded that Grade 4 children, irrespective of gender, who had some choice in selecting a classroom seat at the beginning of the school year, showed differences in spelling ability that were related to whether they sat to the left or to the right of the classroom, facing the teacher. Children on the right were superior spellers, and this held true for their performance on two spelling tests of 50 words each.

The remedial intervention steps proposed in Chapter 3 were designed to develop effective strategies and procedures for overcoming learning disabilities. They are based on understanding the processing differences, the cognitive systems and hemispheric processing modes, and how to utilize information gathered from various sources to develop learning formats that will make a difference in how a child learns in school. These learning and cognitive formats will be further discussed in the ensuing sections of this chapter.

Actual sessions with learning disabled and normal children will be used to provide you with information on how I gather information, test hypotheses, use "test-train-test" procedures and install new cognitive and learning formats. The actual examples illustrate how to make sure that the newly acquired information processing formats are generalized across contexts. As you go through the examples, try to understand my intentions in asking certain questions, and how responses to my questions provide information about the direction you need to go in order to change the learning disabled child's cognitive systems and hemispheric information processing systems. See if you can apply the model presented in Chapters 2 and 3 as a basis for understanding my interventions.

Spelling
John Can't Spell

P = Psychologist
M = Mother
J = John, a Grade 5 student, age 10 years and 4 months

P: I understand that John has a learning problem. Can you give me more information about it?
M: John is a terrible speller. In fact, he can't spell at all! He's been classified as having a serious spelling disability.
P: Has he been in a resource room, or has he received some remedial help?
M: Yes, but they couldn't help him. Both the resource room teacher and his regular classroom teacher said that he'd never be a good speller. As far as they are concerned, he'll always do poorly in spelling, and some children are just born poor spellers.
P: Does his spelling problem affect any other subject area?
M: Yes, John doesn't like to write because he's afraid to make spelling errors. He says he remembers the red marks he received when he tried to write a story.
P: John, you've been sitting there listening to your mom talk about your problem. Do you agree with her?
J: Well, I find it really hard to do. I can't remember how to spell the words when I have a spelling test.
P: I imagine you don't do so well on those tests?
M: That's right. But he can do them the night before the test. He knows them then!
P: How *do* you study for a spelling test, John?
J: I look at the words (*eyes straight ahead*) and repeat them to myself (*eyes down left*). I say them over and over again until I know them (*eyes still down and left*). But when I try to remember them the next day (*eyes up to the right*) I just seem to have forgotten them (*eyes down right*).
P: How do you spell the word "planet"?
J: (*John first looks down and right, then down and left, spelling the word as he continues to look down to the left.*) P-L-A-N-T

P: Are you sure?

J: (*John takes a few seconds to review what he has said by looking down and to the left for some time, and then moving his eyes down and to the right.*) No.

P: How do you spell "hockey"?

J: (*Again John looks down right and then down left.*) H-O K-E.

P: Is that right?

J: (*Looks down, to the left and then to the right.*) I don't know.

P: John, I bet that you sounded the words out inside your head. You said the words to yourself to hear what they sounded like. Is that right? (*As John listens to this description, he looks intently at me and frequently nods his head in response to my assessment.*)

J: Yes.

P: John, can you make pictures inside your head?

J: No.

P: You haven't seen *Star Wars*?

J: Yes, I have!

P: Can you see with your mind's eye (*this expression was explained to him*) what Chewbacca the Wookie looks like? That is, can you see a picture of him inside your head?

J: (*Looks up to the left, eyes dilate, and he stares for a few seconds.*) Yes, I can!

P: What does he look like?

J: (*John again looks up and to the left, pupils dilated.*) He's brown, like mom's old, furry hat. He has a gun across his chest. It's black, I think.

P: Can you see his face clearly?

J: (*Again he looks up to the left, pausing for a few seconds as if he really sees it.*) Yes, it's awfully big.

P: (*Laughs*) Good. Now, John, look at the word "school" on this card. See the whole word. DO NOT SOUND IT OUT. *Now*, take that word and put it into the Wookie's mouth so that whenever you look up there (*I point up to the left and gesture with my own eyes*) you can still see the whole word. In fact, you might want the Wookie to close his mouth and then open it again to *make sure the word is still there*. Tell me when you can *see the whole word clearly*. I want you to *look up there* (*leading John's eyes up to the left by tonal and nonverbal communication*) and spell "school." All you have to do is read it off.

J: S-C-H-O-O-L.

P: Let's spell it a couple more times (*John does so*). Now, John, I'm going to ask you to do something funny, because I want to make sure you are really seeing the word clearly. All right? (*nods*) Spell the word "school" backward.

J: (*John is calm and relaxed. He looks up to the left, pauses a few seconds.*) L-O-O-H-C-S.

P: Now, John, I want you to learn how to spell this next word, "psychology". I know it's a big word but *you can do it.* Now, look at it, see the whole word, and put it in the Wookie's mouth. When you can *see the whole word*, tell me. (*John takes his time, looking at the word and then putting it up into the Wookie's mouth. Finally, after 30 seconds, he says OK.*)

P: Excellent! Now spell it.

J: P-S-Y-C-H-O-L-O-G-Y. (*This was done at a quick pace.*)

P: That's fantastic! You *can* spell. Who said you couldn't! (*John breaks into a smile.*) I want you to spell it a few more times. I want you to look up there, see the word "psychology", and spell it backward.

J: (*John spells it to himself.*) Y-G-O-L-O-H-C-Y-S-P.

M: I can't believe it! I could never do that!

[I continued to teach John how to spell more words, having him first place them in the Wookie's mouth and then spell them out loud. John learned to spell fifteen words.]

P: John, now that you have learned how to spell many words and have proven to me that *you are a speller* - and you will learn to be a very good one at that - I am going to test you on them so that you can take these skills with you. I want you to take these skills so that when you take a spelling test you *remember to look up, see the word, and then spell it.* Immediately I say the word to be spelt I want you to look up there (*gestures*), see the whole word, and then, *and only then*, copy it down on paper. Do you understand that? All right, let's try one.

I had John rehearse the steps of hearing the word, looking up to see the whole word, and then completing the task by writing it down. I then had him look at the written word on his paper, then look up to see it with his mind's eye, and COMPARE IT with what he had written down. John spelt the fifteen words correctly. However, had they not been correct, I would have made him correct the errors either by changing what he had written on the paper or by changing the picture of the word in his mind's eye.

I emphasized to John that it was important for him to spell this way. He was a master of phonics, and now I wanted him to become a master of visualization, a master speller. I recommended that John's mother work with him each night until the newly acquired learning format became as automatic as his old one. He was to return in two weeks.

In two weeks, John returned, his face all aglow. He could hardly contain himself.

J: I got 98 percent on my last spelling test, and 86 on the first one! The teacher was really surprised. I think she thought I was cheating or something, because she kept her eye on me during the test.

From this point on, I worked on refining the spelling strategy, offering John and his mother more information and help in streamlining it. I also talked to John about taking responsibility for learning new words on his own. It was suggested that, as a game, John might learn some new words and then see if he could stump his mother. Each time she failed to spell a word, but John could, then his mother had to pay him 5 cents. John seemed to like that idea.

As a postscript to this case illustration, John is now beginning Grade 6 and his spelling ability has been maintained over two years. There has also been a generalization to his writing ability. His much improved spelling skills have positively affected his attitude toward writing. But to conclude, let's listen to John.

J: I like to write now. I don't make as many errors as before, but when I do I find out how to spell them and then put them up in my friend's mouth. I had to use other images because the Wookie's mouth was getting too full! I feel a lot better about doing it.

Scott
Transcript from a Video Presentation of a Grade 3 Student with a Spelling Dysfunction

The following case illustration is taken from a videotape of a Grade 3 student named Scott. Scott was having extreme difficulty in spelling, and this also manifested itself during writing assignments. The results of the Schonnel Spelling Tests revealed Scott functioned at a pre-Grade 1 level. The case history is presented in great detail so that you can begin to understand how I go about gathering appropriate information, how I use "test-train-test" procedures, and how I use already existing eye-movement patterns and cognitive behaviors to install the spelling format. The transcript is particularly interesting because Scott is very direct and informative about certain difficulties he experiences in learning to generalize the newly acquired spelling format to the regular classroom. He is also very much aware of his own cognitive systems and mental operations, and explicitly details the strategies he employs to spell effectively, as well as the strategies he uses to guess at the spelling of words he does not know or has never previously encountered.

Your are asked to follow the dialogue with care, because there are numerous informative exchanges between Scott and me that can provide some important information about the internal cognitive procedures learning disabled children employ to create ineffective spelling behaviors. Before the actual taping, I could see that Scott was feeling some anxiety. He was told to remain calm and not to look directly at the camera.

P = Psychologist
S = Scott

P: Scott, first I'm going to ask you to spell some words for me. Then I'm going to ask you some questions to *help me understand what you're doing on the inside*; that is, inside your head. All right? The first word I'm going to ask you to spell is "knife".

S: (*Looks up to the left.*) K-I-F-E.

P: Is that right? (*Scott searches up left, down right, up right. He manifests a physiological shift, leans backward on his chair, places his hands in his pockets, and laughs.*)
Go ahead, spell it again out loud and tell me if it's right. I want to know if you know how it's right or not.

S: (*Looks down left, then down right.*) N-I-F-I

P: And how do you spell "teacher"?

S: (*Up left.*) T-E-C-H-E-R (*looks laterally to the left*).

P: How do you spell the word "planet"?

S: P-L-E-N . . . No, I mean A-N (*He looks straight ahead.*)

P: Is that "plan" or "planet"?

S: Oops! I forgot the "t." (*Looks laterally to the left, then up left.*)

P: How do you spell the word "nail"?

S: N-A (*down left, up right, down right, up left*) E-L.

P: How do you spell the word "song"?

S: (*Looks up to the left.*) S-O-I-N-G.

P: Comb?

S: (*Looks down and to the left.*) C-O-M-E.

P: How do you spell the word "shot"?

S: (*Looks down left, and then up left.*) S-H-O-T.

P: Now tell me how you spell the words. What do you do inside your head? Do you try to sound them out? (*Scott looks straight up and responds to the question with a nod of his head.*)

S: Well, I . . . just think (*eyes up straight or straight up*) of the word and then sort of whisper it to myself . . . and all that, and then I just think of the words (*looks up right*) and what it would be, and then I spell it.

P: Scott, when you say you think of the word, do you mean as in trying to say the word to yourself, or by trying to see it?

S: Like trying to see the word (*eyes up right*). Like when I read it, I know what it's like and then (*up right, straight up*) I try to look at it in my head (*eyes up right*).

P: And are the pictures in your head clear?

S: Yeah! (*eyes straight up*)
P: Are they in black and white or are they in color?
S: Black and white.
P: Do you ever make pictures in color?
S: Sometimes.
P: What happens when you do that? Does it make it last longer, or is it easier?
S: It makes it easier to see.
P: Do you also talk to yourself inside your head? When people ask you to spell words, do you ever get a feeling inside you that kind of tells you "Hey, I can't do this"?
S: (*Looks down right.*) Well, it's sort of . . . when I try to think what will it be . . . well, I've never had this word in a while (*up right, down right*). Let's see (*up left, up right*). I then try to guess the word.
P: Oh, I see. You may have seen the word a long time ago, but if you're asked to spell it you realize that it's really kind of new, so you search for it in your head, and if you can't find it you . . .
S: I just go ahead and guess at the letters. I sound out a letter, like 'Z-Z-Z-Z', then I write down all the rest of the letters to see if the word makes sense.
P: How do you *know* if it makes sense?
S: Oh, well, I just try to sound out the vowels (*eyes down left*) and all that, and then I just read it out to myself. If it seems to make sense I say it to myself. If it's wrong, I just try again.
P: Oh, so it makes sense when you sound it out. If it sounds right, it makes sense to you? When you sound out a word like knife . . .
S: Yes, I just do the same thing (*looks down, up right*). I say an 'e' at first, and then (*looks up right*) I say an 'i' and that makes sense.
P: Would you like to spell more effectively?
S: Well, I'd like to hear the word and then spell it out.
P: Just give it out, right? Do you understand, Scott, that *good spellers do not sound out the word?* When someone says a word, they go inside their head and make *a picture* and *see it* and read it out. Did you *know that?*
S: Usually it's hard to do that sometimes (*eyes up right and then straight up*).
P: What makes it hard to do that?
S: You're thinking (*eyes down left*). You see it (*eyes up right*) in your head, and then you think it could be wrong (*eyes down right*), so . . .
P: So, when you look at it and see it in your head, you kind of say to yourself, it's wrong?
S: It might be wrong, or it might be right.

P: So, you really don't know at this point how to determine whether it's right or wrong? (*nods*) Good! Now I want you just to *look* up (*points up left*) . . . you go up to look. Can you see the word "knife" there (*points as Scott nods*) Can you read it backward?

S: (*Scott looks straight up.*) E-F-I-N-F?

P: I-N-F? *Look* up and *spell it* backward.

S: Oh, (*looks up*) E-F-E-N-K.

P: Look up there (*points up left*) and spell it backward again. OK, now you go up there, see it clearly . . .

S: Oh, wow! (*eyes straight up, slightly to the left*) I can see it clearly!

P: Spell it.

S: K-N-I-F-E.

P: Now spell it backward.

S: E-F-I-N-K.

P: Fantastic! Great! If you could *do that all the time*, spelling would be easy for you.

S: But usually our teacher doesn't let us look at our sheets (*looks straight up*).

P: Well, we need to teach you to look up there, because whenever you look up there it is very important for you to see the word clearly. When you looked up there, You even said, "Oh wow! It's clear!" It *was* clear, wasn't it?

S: Well, the first few times (*up slightly to the right*) I could just see it in black and white bits . . . but it was blurry.

P: So now when you look at the word "knife" . . .

S: It's easy.

P: All right look up there and . . . look at it again and tell me if it's clear.

S: (*Looks straight up.*) Yes.

P: Is it in color?

S: No.

P: What would happen if you put it in color? Put it in *your favorite color* . . . up there. You see the knife, and then you put the word "knife" on the handle in your favorite color. Now, tell me a word you can spell.

S: (*Eyes down left*) Grandmama.

P: How do you spell Grandmama?

S: G-R-A-N-M-A-M-A.

P: Try again.

S: (*Eyes up right, down left, down right.*) G-R-A-N-D-M-A-M-A.

P: Is that right? (*Scott acknowledges nonverbally*) Now, tell me another word that you can spell.

S: B-A-G. Bag.

P: How do you know "bag" is right?

S: Cause I've known it (*eyes up left*) for a long time.

P: Yes, but something on the inside must tell you or show you that it's right.

S: Well, I look at the picture (*nonverbally uses his hands to outline a square*). They say 'bag' and I just picture that bag in my head. I look at that word on it and I say it.

P: So you see the bag inside your head, see the word on it, and then read the word? (*As I was speaking, Scott acknowledged nonverbally that what I was saying matched his internal process for knowing how to spell the word "bag".*) Good idea! Ever try to do that with other words? Like "knife". Picture a knife in your head and see the word "knife" written on it?

S: Well, that hasn't happened to me yet. I haven't seen a knife (*nonverbal gestures accompany his response*) with the word "knife" written on it!

P: Well you can do it in your own head. (*Scott nods*) See if you can make a picture of a knife inside your head. (*Scott looks up right and then up left.*) You got it? (*nods*) Put, right on the handle, the word "knife", K-N-I-F-E. (*Scott looks up right and then straight up.*) Make it clear. Even put it in color, if you have to. Now, look at that picture again. How do you spell the word "knife"?

S: (*Looks up and left.*) K-N-I-F-E (*straight up*).

P: Good for you! Now I'm going to give you a tough word. It's called "psychology" (*points to the word on a flash card*).

S: (*Looks at the word.*) Psychology.

P: I want you to make a picture of the whole word, but DON'T SAY THE LETTERS TO YOURSELF. Scott, pretend that your mind is like a camera . . . read the letters to me.

[I already knew one procedure that would work with Scott. I now show him a word placed on a flash card held up to the left to determine if he can learn how to spell through a slightly different format that requires simultaneous visual-spatial processes. I have decided to attack Scott's weak areas directly, rather than employ his strong auditory-phonetic-cognitive processes.]

P: Look at the word on this flash card. Take a snapshot of the whole word. Good! I'm going to take the flash card away. Now, see the whole word. Can you see it?

S: (*Looks up, slightly to the left.*) Yes.

P: Spell it.

S: P-S-Y-O-G-L-O. Whoops! I got up the line and knew I forgot the "ch."

P: That's OK. Look at it again, and this time learn only the first five letters, and then the next five letters.
    (*Scott looks at the word and then moves his eyes straight up; looks at the word again and again moves his eyes straight up.*)

P: That's the way. Do you have it?

S: P-S-Y-C-H-O-L-O-G-Y.

P: Fantastic! I want you to look up there and see the word "psychology", then put it in your favorite color and spell it out for me.

S: (*Scott looks up to see the word, puts it in his favorite color and then practices it out loud* [subvocalization].) OK, P-S-Y-C-H-O-L-O-G-Y.

P: Look at it again. Take a snapshot. Do it as you did it before. Look at it, move your eyes up there and then come back and check it against the flash card. Can you see all the letters? Are they the same as on the card? (*nods*) All right, spell it for me.

S: (*Eyes straight up.*) P-S-Y-C-H-O-L-O-G-Y.

P: Good! Look up there again. Do it again, and this time, as you say it out loud, the picture is going to get a lot brighter and you will be able to see it a lot clearer.

S: (*Eyes straight up.*) P-S-Y-C-H-O-L-O-G-Y.

P: I want you now to look at that picture up there. It's pretty bright, isn't it? (*Scott looks up and nods.*) It's clear? (*nods*) Now spell it backward. What is the last letter?

S: Y.

P: Next?

S: (*Looks straight up.*) Y-G-O-L-O-H-C-Y-S-P.

P: Great! Isn't it *neat* to be able *to do that?* Now I'm going to show you something: something I want you to learn how to do. I want you to spell a couple of words for me. The first word is "knife", but before you spell it . . . BEFORE YOU SPELL IT . . . I want you to look up and see the picture of the word "knife" and then just copy it down on the paper. (*Scott does so.*) Now, look at that picture of the word "knife" up there and *compare it* with the word you wrote down on your paper. Are the two words the same? (*nods*) Look up there, see the word "psychology" and copy it down. (*Scott looks up frequently.*) Now what I want you to do is to look at the written word and the picture of it up there, and check the letters to see if they are both the same.

S: They're the same.

P: Let's play around with some other words. How do you spell the word "comb"?

S: (*Looks up and to the right.*) C-O-M-E.

P: All right. Now, Scott, I want you to look up there and make a picture of a comb. Got it? (*Scott nods.*) Good. Now, on the handle write the word "comb", C-O-M-B. See it clearly. Put it in your favorite color so that it's bright and clear. (*Scott moves his eyes straight up, takes his time and nods.*) Good. Spell it.

S: Scott looks straight up and says "C-O-M-B."

From here on, the video shows me teaching Scott how to spell other words, making sure that he knows the process and spelling format well. Once it was obvious from nonverbal feedback cues, I had Scott learn several words by himself, then tested him on all twelve words he had learned. Scott performed perfectly, frequently looking up without being instructed to do so, to find the pictures of the words. When it became clear that Scott was using the new spelling strategy automatically, I taught Scott how to use it in his classroom. He was reminded that when the teacher asked him to spell a word, he was first to look up and see the whole word, and then write it down on paper. After writing it down, he was to compare what he had written with what he saw up above and ask himself if the words were exactly alike.

I was fortunate in the sense that Scott's teacher had attended one of my workshops, so when she was asked to monitor Scott's progress and make certain that he automatically looked up and that he pictured the whole word, she readily agreed. (She occasionally had to remind him to look up.)

The teacher's follow-up revealed that Scott was doing exceptionally well on his spelling tests, obtaining grades in the nineties to one hundred. The year-end results on the Canadian Tests of Basic Skills placed Scott at a middle Grade 3 level. The results of the Schonnel Spelling Test placed him at an early Grade 4. Not only was Scott happy with his progress, so were his parents. His dad had expressed the opinion that Scott would always be a poor speller since he himself had never been able to spell!

Both case illustrations are examples of learning disabled students who exhibited spelling dysfunctions with varying degrees of severity. The procedures used to install the spelling format, the new cognitive strategy, have proven to be successful in teaching learning disabled students how to spell more effectively. However, there remains a small percentage of students who seem unable to create internal imagery, to make pictures inside their heads. For the most part, these students have the innate ability to generate internal pictures but, for whatever reason, they seem simply to have shut down that cognitive system. Yet their accessing cues suggest that they are quite capable of making internal pictures at an unconscious level. This implies that the use of visualization cognitive processes is outside their conscious awareness. Further inquiry into this interesting phenomenon reveals that most of these children dream in vivid images and describe their perceptual position as being outside the image, looking in at themselves. A significant number of these students have very frequent nightmares. One other characteristic of these children seems to be associated with early childhood trauma in which they saw things that really frightened them. Perhaps, at an unconscious level, they deliberately suppressed the use of internal pictures so that they could dissociate themselves from painful memories. It is also interesting that many of these children are almost predisposed to ignore the visual aspects of their environment.

The latter group of children represents a very small percentage. In most cases, children can be taught directly how to create or generate internal imagery. If the teaching is approached in an atmosphere of fun and games, most students learn very quickly and effectively. For some students, you may need to employ techniques designed to elicit and generate internal visualization processes. This can be accomplished by employing the psychological phenomena of after-images. You can present the learning disabled student with examples of after-images that are often portrayed in introductory psychology textbooks. Or, you can make up your own by placing letters of different colors against a different-colored background. The contrast between foreground and background hues will generate an after-image effect when the learning disabled student looks at it for thirty seconds and then closes his eyes. As the learning disabled student closes his eyes, he should become aware of an internal image produced by the external stimulus. For some students, the internal image may be fuzzy or hazy, and this feedback should be taken as a good sign. This, of course, represents the first stage in teaching learning disabled students how to construct, develop and maintain internal visual imagery. The ability to see clear, internal pictures, to think imagistically, must be activated and developed by other specialized techniques (Houston, 1982).

While specialized techniques requiring sophisticated electronic instrumentation and advanced technology exist to generate and develop internal visualization processes, other, more basic, psychological procedures can produce equally effective results.

One such technique that has proven useful and successful in helping learning disabled students activate, generate and develop the ability to imagine/think in pictures is called "bridging." The procedure involves using the learning disabled child's strongest cognitive system as a pivotal point for expanding and developing the other, less well developed representational mental processes. In other words, the teacher must first identify the student's most preferred cognitive system. Second, the teacher must determine which target (desired) state should be developed in order to make a difference in how that student learns. Third, the educator must pace and match the learning disabled student's strongest system and identify the means for bridging it to another, less well developed cognitive system.

The means for bridging the present state (the strongest cognitive system) to the desired state (the less well developed representational system) can be likened to an exercise in guided imagery.

For example, one creative resource room teacher who attempted to apply the spelling format outlined in this chapter, quickly realized that the learning disabled student she was working with lacked the cognitive ability to generate the internal imagery of words. No matter what procedure she used, the student still could not construct an internal image of the stimulus word. Somewhat nonplussed by this learning deficiency, she recalled the data collected about this student's internal processing preferences. His postural responses, head tilts, breathing patterns, eye movements and predicate words identified him as a kinesthetic learner and processor. Using this knowledge, she told him to look up and to the left, and to identify visually a letter she would write on his back. In other words, he was to take the kinesthetic input and translate it into a visual representation of the letter. As she drew the letter on his back, and as he adapted to the feel of it, he began to see the outline of the letter. Once he could see it clearly, he would vocalize which letter it was and then receive appropriate feedback. In an atmosphere of fun and learning, that learning disabled student was able to develop the ability to see words inside his head. In fact, the experience led to the same student developing other abilities, such as seeing characters and settings internally; a skill that came in handy for developing his reading comprehension.

Bridging is a very powerful technique for developing any cognitive system that is less well developed than the other mental processes. It can also be employed within a guided imagery format (Bry, 1978; DeMille, 1973; Hershey, 1979; Khatena, 1979; Lowenfels, 1979; Prichard, 1980). As an educator, you can employ guided imagery with an individual student or group of students who may not be able to employ a particular cognitive system as part of the thinking process. You can also employ this format with a whole class, as long as you have the sensory acuity to use feedback.

One other technique that seems to work effectively in teaching children how to visualize inside their heads is a game called "Camera." One simply requests that the student think of his brain as comparable to a camera. As a camera, the student's brain is quite capable of taking snapshots of external objects or things and then letting the picture develop inside his head. The procedure can be reinforced by actually showing students how the unfolding process takes place. Once they have an external example of the process they can begin to play the game of camera.

The game requires two people to be partners. Partner one will lead partner two around the room, outside, or anywhere, but the second partner must keep his eyes closed until the leader gives him a signal to open them and take a snapshot of whatever is directly in front. The signal can take the form of the first student grasping the partner's wrist and squeezing it when it is time for him to open his eyes to take a snapshot. Approximately thirty seconds after partner two has taken a snapshot of some external object, he again closes his eyes and describes in great detail what he sees inside his head. Then, he opens his eyes again and compares his internal image with the actual stimulus object, noting the differences and the similarities. He then closes his eyes once more to see if he can obtain a more complete internal picture of the object. Partner one, depending on his level of sophistication, can ask relevant questions to elicit a more complete and accurate description of the stimulus picture. He might, for example, ask if the internal image is in color or black and white, if it is big, small, life-size, or greater than life-size; what the shape of the external object is like, and if it appears close by or far away.

Partner one continues to lead partner two around, taking all kinds of internal snapshots of his external environment. Then, after a number of enriching experiences, he is either brought back to the classroom to draw a picture of one of his snapshots in as complete detail as possible, or the partners can switch places, so that both have had the chance to experience this procedure. Afterward, both partners can go back to the classroom and each draw a picture of one of their snapshots. The sketches or drawings should be as detailed as possible. Perhaps, after completing their pictures, the partners can compare their renditions with the original stimulus objects.

Each day, the classroom teacher could reinforce this skill by having the students look at pictures for fifteen seconds, close their eyes and then draw from memory what they see within their minds or with their mind's eye. The classroom teacher may want to teach children some of the basics of drawing. One researcher (Brookes, 1986) concluded that teaching children how to draw was correlated with improvements in academic achievement. The reason this finding may be accurate is best described by Brookes (1986:xiii) when she states: "She taught us how to gather information visually, elaborate on it mentally, and express it manually. She taught us a thinking process, how to analyze anything we saw so that we could draw it."

This process taught children to appreciate the pictorial aspects of their environment and to think in terms of visual images (McKim, 1972). The potentiated internal ability provides them with more cognitive distinctions in their sensory systems, a process which is analogous to increasing the number of books in one's personal library. The more books you own, the more knowledge you will have at your disposal. Adding more books to your library, however, does little good if they are not read or used in practical ways.

Similar experiences can be provided for children to enable them to develop greater cognitive distinctions in their auditory and kinesthetic sensory systems. Children can learn to appreciate distinctions of tone, timbre, tempo, pitch, and volume distinctions in the cognitive system. They can, for example, learn to listen to pieces of their favorite musical compositions and identify instruments based on the sounds heard throughout each musical piece. In the kinesthetic mode, they can learn to estimate weight based on the feel of certain objects. They can learn to discriminate tactile differences in a variety of materials and substances. Learning disabled students, too, can learn to develop a higher level of cognitive flexibility by translating one sensory system into another one. Such synthesia or cross-modal patterning could form the basis for developing more cognitive distinctions. It could affect a child's ability to learn in various subject areas. Many exercises could be developed within the classroom or the resource room to facilitate the development of cross-modal processing.

Having students listen to music and translate it into colors or images, or into feelings, teaches them how to understand the concept of synthesia and its importance to learning. Further exercises could be developed to teach them how to translate feelings (tactile or kinesthetic) into images or sounds. Or, they could be taught to translate colors or images into sounds and feelings. More complex cognitive distinctions could be developed by having children learn to hold two or more sensory systems simultaneously in their mind, and this could be generalized to subject areas such as mathematics, reading or problem solving.

Rationale for the Spelling Strategy

A number of researchers have considered reading and spelling abilities to be interrelated and relying on similar cognitive processes (Boder, 1971; Markoff, 1979; Nelson & Warrington, 1976; Reitan, 1984), while other investigators have treated them as separate skills (Reitan, 1984; Rourke, 1983; Sweeny and Rourke, 1978) employing differential hemispheric styles. Myklebust (1975), for example, postulated two types of learning disabled students: those with verbal-linguistic deficits in the left hemisphere, and those with visual-spatial deficiencies associated with the right hemisphere. This was generalized to include spelling patterns associated with dysfunctions in the left and the right hemispheres (Boder, 1971; Myklebust, 1978; Reitan, 1984; Rourke and Finlayson, 1978; Rourke and Strang, 1978; Rourke, 1985; Strang and Rourke, 1983).

The spelling strategy/format outlined in this chapter relies primarily on right-hemispheric cognitive processes. The fact that the learning disabled student must orient his eyes and his head to the left presupposes that there is an activation of sensory systems (visual) associated with the contralateral right hemisphere (Kinsbourne, 1972, 1974; Levy and Reid, 1976, 1978; Moscovitch and Smith, 1979; Wittrock, 1978). The spelling format relies on the student's ability to synthesize the letters or syllables into larger units or ''chunks''; it requires the activation of the gestalt visual function associated with the right brain (Chall & Myrsky, 1978). To be able to see the whole word depends on the ability to visualize the entire configuration internally and to be able to move into the synthetic mode of cognitive functioning.

Recent research (Flaro, 1986, 1987/88) supports the effectiveness of the spelling format. Further research is in progress (Flaro, in press) and preliminary results confirm its usefulness and effectiveness in remedying spelling dysfunctions in learning disabled students. The application of the spelling strategy by resource room teachers (Flaro, 1987/88) and several classroom teachers (Flaro, in press), with Grade 3 students, has also confirmed its effectiveness by statistically improving spelling performance.

TABLE 4
The Spelling Format: Procedural Steps

Step 1.
Before proceeding to install the spelling format, you need to ask the learning disabled student questions to determine where he looks to access eidetic imagery or past visually remembered information. This is done by paying attention to the FIRST initial eye movement the student makes when responding to your questions. In this situation, you need to use visual representational words designed to stimulate visual memory. Your questions should be in the past tense to prompt clean and crisp eye-movement patterns: they should presuppose the existence of past visual memories or experiences and be sensory specific in terms of representational cognitive systems. Questions such as: What was the color of your Grade 1 teacher's hair? What was the color of the first room you remember? or, When you were very young, what color of hair did you have? are examples designed to draw forth the desired response.

The questions cited presuppose the accessing of visually remembered information. They will elicit characteristic eye movements that should tell you where a child codes past visual imagery. You will find, however, that some learning disabled students have characteristic eye movements in other quadrants, depending on their preferred cognitive and hemispheric modes of functioning, and that they don't seem to access up and to the left. Please remember, children who prefer to talk to themselves will tend to access down and to the left, and, even though you ask for an internal visual image, they may, in fact,

TABLE 4 (Continued)

verbally label it (repeat it to themselves) and tell you that they can see the picture clearly! Similarly, students who organize information kinesthetically may look down and to the right to get a feel for the word, or to write it out on their leg. Also, some children, especially learning disabled children, frequently look down and to the right because this behaviorally nominalized posture is closely associated with beliefs about their learning abilities as well as being directly linked to their own self-perceptions.

Usually, in normally right-handed students, it is safe to conclude that language functions are located in the left hemisphere, while visual-spatial abilities are associated with the right cerebral cortex. This presupposition underlies the spelling format and will predispose the teacher to hold a flash card to the learning disabled child's upper left quadrant. While this position will be effective in many cases, it is still you, the educator, whose responsibility it is to make sure certain that this is in fact the case; otherwise, the procedure will not have a long-term effect.

Step 2.

Use flash cards showing appropriate spelling words: these words can be taken from a Schonnell or Dolch list, or from the learning disabled student's grade level reader. In either case, the words chosen must be at the child's current level of spelling ability. For some learning disabled students, it is much more effective if the words are written in specific colors, or if the vowels are put in specific colors. If the learning disabled student has trouble with reversals, then the letters can be written in different colors.

Place the flash card to the learning disabled student's upper left quadrant, a position that should be comfortable for him. Have him look at the word until he can SEE THE WHOLE WORD with his mind's eye. This implies that the learning disabled student will not be using any internal dialogue or subvocalizations to remember the word. You must also stop any use of phonics. Once the learning disabled student can see the whole word, flip the flash card over and have him continue to SEE IT on the blank side of the card, or with his mind's eye, as he continues to LOOK UP AND TO THE LEFT. At first, some children may need to close their eyes to gain access to the internal image of the stimulus word. When the student can SEE IT, have him SPELL IT by reading it off the internal picture. If he can't see the word, then repeat the process. Because success at this stage is important for the student, make certain that the first word the learning disabled student is to learn is within his level of spelling performance.

Step 3.

Once the student can spell the word, then you need to TEST whether

TABLE 4 (Continued)

or not he can visualize the word with his mind's eye. To do this, have him SPELL IT BACKWARD. (To insure that you understand the significance of this remedial procedure, spell the word "psychology" backward!) Clinical experience suggests that children who can spell words backward at a good clip are indeed visualizing the word. You can tell if a child is actually saying a word to himself by noting the length of time it takes to spell the stimulus word, or you can watch for subvocalizing mouth movements. These behaviors need to be stopped (unless you can make use of them) since the student is engaging in phonemic processes as well as using left-hemispheric processes.

Similarly, if the learning disabled student moves his eyes to other quadrants as you ask him to spell a word, then you know that the word is not yet stored in a visual representational system. In this case, have him look up and left again and to SEE THE WORD CLEARLY THIS TIME. You also need to stop wandering eye movements since this indicates that the child is resorting to his old spelling patterns. You want him to LOOK UP LEFT SO THAT HIS RIGHT HEMISPHERE CAN BE ENGAGED and is, therefore, involved in seeing the whole configuration or gestalt of the stimulus word. Once the learning disabled student has accomplished this task successfully, then have him repeat it with several other words.

Step 4.
The next step is to have the learning disabled student use the spelling strategy/format to write on paper the words to be spelled. When you ask him to spell a word, he is immediately to look up and left to see the whole word. After this, he simply copies the word down on paper. If he forgets how to spell it, then GENTLY guide his eyes up and left and ask him to SEE IT AGAIN. If he still can't remember the word to be spelled, then return to Step 2. However, you may wish, at this time, to ask him what you could do to make it easier for him to remember the word. This may mean that you have to make the word brighter or larger. Some children may need the letters to be small enough for them to see the whole configuration of a word. In fact, some children learn to see the whole word, but when you ask them to spell it, they focus in on only one letter at a time and forget the rest! Your task is to do whatever it takes to make sure the student sees the whole word and that he can stabilize this image when he spells it, either vocally or in writing.

Step 5.
When the student has written a word down on paper, have him look up and left again, SEE THE WHOLE WORD and COMPARE IT with what he has written down on paper. Ask him if the two are exactly the same. If he says no, then have him correct the mistake either with his mind's

TABLE 4 (Continued)

eye or on paper. If his answer is yes, then reinforce his NEW SPELLING ABILITIES! This procedure builds in an internal/external comparison process; a reference structure for KNOWING when a word is spelled either correctly or incorrectly. Many learning disabled students do not have an internal reference system for determining whether something is right or wrong (Feurstein, 1980).

Step 6.
Sometimes, as a supplemental procedure, the resource room teacher, as well as the regular classroom teacher, can have the learning disabled student see the spelling word in his favorite color. This helps to reinforce his visual representational system capabilities. Some students respond best to this procedure when it is explained that their mind is like a camera and that it can take still snapshots of THE WHOLE WORD. Don't be too surprised if some students take this suggestion literally and you begin to notice that the student is blinking frequently! This simply means that he is performing the task accurately and his blinks are being used to represent the camera's shutter action.

Step 7.
Once a student has successfully spelled a number of words, the resource, remedial or regular classroom teacher should repeat the process as often as possible until the spelling format becomes an unconsciously applied program. You will know when this point is reached because, on being asked to spell a word, the learning disabled student's response will be like that of a very good speller: there will be an automatic up and left eye movement. This external behavioral cue provides you with FEEDBACK about the progress the student is making and the degree to which the spelling format is an improvement over the student's previous spelling pattern. The teacher needs to emphasize to the learning disabled student that if he can't spell a word, then he should still look up and left to see it. This specific information reinforces to the student that he has metacognitive awareness and control over his representational systems, and provides him with relevant information about how to use this awareness to retrieve or re-access a learned word. In this way, you begin to shift the student's behavioral locus of control and provide the student with the means to become an exceptionally good speller.

Step 8.
The final step is to ensure that the learning disabled student has generalized the new spelling format sufficiently for use in the classroom. For many learning disabled students, the process needs to be taught specifically and directly. If it is possible, you need to include the classroom teacher in this remedial procedure. The teacher could then

TABLE 4 (Continued)

reinforce the student's new spelling format in the classroom by reminding him to look up and left to see the whole word, copy it down, and
then evaluate whether or not it is correct. The teacher could also make
certain that the student uses the spelling procedure to learn new words
on his spelling list. With this type of feedback, the learning disabled
student will quickly learn the format and eventually use it as a matter
of habit.

   For various reasons, it may not be possible to include the classroom
teacher in reinforcing the student's new spelling format, in which case
you will need to use guided imagery to teach him, and show him how
to use the strategy for himself in the classroom. You have to show him
how to see himself in the classroom *just before he is going to take
a spelling test*. Have him sit at his desk, make himself comfortable (if
you know about anchoring, then use this technique), and then listen
to the teacher's voice as she gives the class a word to spell. Once he
hears the word, he is automatically to look up and left, see the whole
word, copy it down and check its accuracy. Have him run through several scenarios, engaging as many representational systems as possible,
so that he can bring the new resource into the classroom and use it.
Have him repeat the process until he believes he can perform in exactly the same way within as without the classroom.

Creative Writing

   The following discussion took place between two Grade 12 students and myself. I was seeing Rachelle because of her poor writing
skills in language arts. Her written work was characterized by teachers
as being disorganized, logically inconsistent and disjointed. Apparently, her thoughts would jump from one point to another without
any internal consistency between them. Yet, Rachelle was highly motivated to learn the skills required to become an effective writer, as well
as to be able to pass her Grade 12 examinations.

   Prior to this particular meeting with Rachelle, I had been working
with her, teaching her how to employ visualization processes to gather
appropriate information, how to use her eye-movement patterns to
access resourceful internal strengths, and how to generate verbal output. In the latter area, I attempted to teach her how to connect her
internal images with words. Over ten sessions, she progressed at a
moderate rate. From September to December of 1986 she managed
to increase her overall classroom average from 51 percent to 65 percent. This improvement was encouraging to Rachelle as well as to
her Grade 12 language arts teacher. It was also the minimal grade she
needed to be accepted in pharmacology at a neighboring university!

   Still, Rachelle wanted to pursue her newly acquired writing skills
and to improve them. During one of the sessions she stated that a

friend of hers was an exceptional writer, always receiving marks in the nineties on written essays and papers. I suggested to Rachelle that maybe Andrea would be willing to come to the next session to discuss her writing strategy, so that Rachelle could incorporate some of the steps into her own newly acquired strategy. What follows is illustrative of Andrea's creative writing strategy. Through questioning, I elicited the strategy and then taught it to Rachelle. Rachelle watched this session with curiosity and excitement, all the while mentally trying out Andrea's strategy.

Andrea's Learning Format

P = Psychologist
A = Andrea
R = Rachelle

I took some time to develop rapport with Andrea by talking to her about school and her extracurricular involvements. Andrea was very friendly and we discussed some of the concepts that Rachelle had learned and employed to increase her writing ability. Andrea was fascinated with this.

P: Andrea, Rachelle tells me that you are extremely proficient at writing, and that you consistently earn marks in the nineties on your written papers and essays. I guess you like to write?
A: Yes, I do. I find writing really easy and can usually complete a paper in no time.
P: I asked Rachelle to invite you to this session because we would like to know what strategy you use to write. That is, when you decide to write about something, what do you do inside your head that enable you to write so well?
A: I don't know. I just think about it (*eyes up to the left*) and then write it.
P: Would you be willing to experiment a little, so that we can begin to understand the cognitive processes you use to be such a good writer?
A: Sure!
P: I'm going to give you a topic to write about, and I want you to develop a story or essay on that topic. Once you have some ideas firmly in your mind, I may ask you to write out your story or essay. The topic is COMPUTERS.
A: (*Andrea looks up and to the left, then down to the left. This eye movement pattern continues for several minutes and then she looks up and right, then down and right, and, finally, looks directly at me.*) OK., I know what I would write about computers.

P: As soon as I gave you the topic of computers, what did you do inside your head?

A: I just thought about it!

P: When you thought about it, did you make a picture inside your head, talk to yourself, or have some particular feeling?

A: I remembered all I knew about computers, and then began to think about what aspect of computers I wanted to write about. I thought of the different types of computers and how they work, my experiences with computers at school, and what others think about this new technology. (*During this discussion, Andrea frequently looked up and to the left.*)

P: So, you thought about past information and experiences with computers, and remembered them by forming a picture inside your head?

A: Yes, I made a big mental picture of all the things I knew about computers. I could see myself using the computers at school, and the teacher telling us how they worked. I also saw myself reading the textbooks on computers, and remembered what those authors had written about them.

P: Well, tell me about the picture inside your head. Was it bigger than life-size? Was it in color? Was it bright?

A: It was quite big, but general. It was not overly bright, but it was in color, although the colors were not that clear.

P: So this was a general picture that incorporated your knowledge of computers?

A: Yes, that's right. I saw all the things I could write about.

P: Once you saw this overall, general picture, what else did you do inside your head?

A: (*Andrea looks up and left and then down to the left.*) Well, I began to ask myself questions about the aspects of computers I would like to write about.

P: Well, how *did* you know what you wanted to write on this topic?

A: Hmm. (*She looks up and left and then down to her left.*) When I asked myself a question I made the picture smaller. The more questions I asked myself, the smaller the picture became.

P: What happened to the picture as it got smaller? What let you know that this picture represented what you wanted to write about?

A: Oh, as the picture got smaller, it became brighter. I also think that I feel more intensely about the picture as it gets smaller. The brighter and the smaller the picture gets the more emotional feelings I have. When the picture gets really bright and emotionally intense, I know then that that is what I want to write about.

P: Let me see if I understand the process you went through to gather information about what to write, given this imposed topic. When I gave you the topic of computers, you looked up there and saw a picture, a general picture, which is quite big, of all the things you knew about computers. (*To this point, Andrea has been nodding to signify that what I was describing was relatively accurate.*) Then you began to ask yourself questions about what part of this big picture you would like to write about (*nods*). As soon as you asked your questions, the big picture became smaller and brighter and had more feelings attached to it. (*Andrea nods, and then smiles.*) The more questions you asked yourself, the smaller the picture became, and the more intense the feelings, until it was just right. That is, it had to be a certain brightness and feel "just right" before you knew what aspect of computers you would write about (*nods*). What I don't understand is what questions did you ask yourself to cause the internal picture to become smaller?

A: (*Looks down and left.*) I asked myself what information I remembered about computers, and I could see myself reading my textbook. I then remembered that my teacher had taught us how to use computers, and so I recalled my experiences learning to understand and operate them. I also asked myself what other experiences I had had that involved computers, and I remembered being over at my friend's house playing with their Apple computer. Next, I asked myself how other people must feel toward learning to use the computer. At this point, my picture became the smallest of all, and I really felt that this was the area I wanted to write about.

P: Now that you know what you are going to write about, how do you go about it?

A: Well, this may sound funny, but that small picture becomes my starting point. I use it as the means for generating my introductory paragraph. I also know how I want my story to end, so I guess I have an ending picture as well.

P: So the small picture becomes the starting point. Then somehow you develop an end slide or picture because you know how it is going to end. Then what do you do?

A: Well, it literally unfolds before me. I fill in the space between the starting picture and the end picture and write about what I see unfolding before my eyes. So, I fill in the middle part between the beginning and end pictures.

P: This is incredible! You literally take the small picture and make it your first slide, so to speak, and you also generate an end slide or picture. Then you somehow fill in the space between the first and the last pictures with more slides. (*Andrea nods and smiles.*) Next, you write about what you see unfolding before your eyes. It's almost descriptive of a movie unfolding, but before it's completed it is a series of frames. How do you know that the story follows logically?

A: Well, after I finish writing, I read the story aloud or whisper the words to myself, and watch the movie! If the story is coherent, the movie runs without a break. If there is a problem, the slide that doesn't follow coherently whites out! Whenever I see a slide whiting out, I know that the story is weak at that spot, so I go back and rewrite until there is no more whiting out. As soon as the story is corrected, I can then watch the whole movie without interruption.

P: You white out! Can you explain this further.

A: Well, as I read the story I watch the movie unfold inside my head. If the story runs smoothly I see the whole thing happening before my eyes. If there is a problem, such as two slides not being connected, the movie begins to turn white until I can't see it anymore. As soon as I become aware that this is happening, I stop reading to see what doesn't fall together. I reread the story, or essay, and determine where the problem lies. Then I correct it and read again, but out loud. If the movie proceeds smoothly, I know I have corrected the problem.

P: Rachelle, you have listened to this and watched Andrea carefully. What did you learn?

R: Well, as soon as you gave Andrea the topic, she looked up there (*points to Andrea's left*) and saw something. Then she looked down here to her left. Then she looked back up there, and again looked down here. This continued for some time. I guess she was seeing pictures in her head and then talking to herself about them. What you taught me to do inside my head is similar to what she does, but I sure have a lot to learn. Can I learn her strategy?

P: Yes, you can, and we'll teach you how to do that in a later session. Andrea, do you have any questions?

A: No, except that I didn't realize all the things I do in my head when I write an essay or paper. It's fascinating. No wonder Rachelle has improved so much in her writing!

P: Thank you, Andrea, for helping us.

Andrea's creative writing strategy represents a sophisticated learning format; integrating a variety of cognitive processes (Bloom's taxonomy, 1956) and the blending of left and right hemispheric functions. Moreover, her cognitive learning format illustrates the complex development and interaction of psychoneurological mechanism, including interneurosensory, intraneurosensory and integrative neurosensory mental processes and modes of functioning.

Observations of Andrea's external behavioral responses (eye movements, head tilts, hand gestures) and questions about her internal, covert cognitive processes revealed a surprising relationship between the two. The results seemed to corroborate Kinsbourne's (1972) research findings suggesting that these behavioral parameters reflect cerebral cognitive processes. Interestingly enough, Andrea did not seem to have the metacognitive awareness of her internal cognitive processes, but, as the author began to ask her sensory-specific questions about what she did inside her head, she responded with surprise and satisfaction at understanding these internal cognitive operations.

There is no question that Andrea has mastered a highly complex process; one of the highest forms of language development. This form of expressive language process, in conjunction with the employment of the visual symbol system to convey an individual's thoughts, feelings and ideas, is certainly evident in Andrea's creative writing strategy. She definitely incorporates the cognitive processes outlined in Bloom's (1956) taxonomy of educational objectives, ranging from the application of learned knowledge to analysis and synthesis of facts and relationships, to the evaluation of the finished product. Not only does writing require an individual to keep an idea in mind, but to order the idea in some sequential relationship (Myklebust, 1965) requires the integration of visual and auditory information usually associated with left and right hemispheric cognitive functions.

In effect, to generate ideas and thoughts in written form, an individual must first know what he wants to write. He must employ past knowledge structures and understand how these can be brought to bear on the present topic (Bloom's knowledge, comprehension and application objectives). Next, the individual must have the ability to formulate and arrange sentences to convey a particular meaning over time (comprehension, analysis). Further, the individual must have the ability to synthesize the discrete cognitive informational units into an integrated whole. This means that the individual must be able to select the relevant information from past knowledge structures and then put them together into a conceptual whole. Once he has some awareness and direction about how to put his thoughts and ideas together, he can begin the task of writing. Finally, he needs the capacity to evaluate his work: to edit, proofread, and revise.

What follows are two brief sessions with a Grade 1 student and a Grade 5 student. Both sessions were transcribed from a video recording. Melissa is a Grade 1 student with average creative writing ability. But, as you read over her transcript you will be able to see the beginning of cognitive processes in terms of mental modes of functioning that are similar to Andrea's cognitive strategy. Melissa's learning format incorporates visual and auditory cognitive processes; left and right hemispheric processes and, possibly, some of Bloom's taxonomy (see Table 5).

Kristin is a Grade 5 student with fairly well-developed language abilities. She is very good at creative writing. She is also a very good

TABLE 5
A Simplified Diagram of
Bloom's Taxonomy of Cognitive Processes

In Bloom's taxonomy, the developmental skills are hierarchial, moving from the simplest cognitive competencies (knowledge, etc.) to the more complex cognitive operations (analysis, synthesis, integration, etc.).

EVALUATION

Evaluation involves the use of criteria or standards for appraising the effectiveness of one's performance.

SYNTHESIS
Synthesis refers to the ability to put things together to form a whole or Gestalt.

ANALYSIS

Analysis is the ability to break complex wholes into smaller, digestible chunks.

APPLICATION
This refers to an individual's ability to generalize past information or knowledge, and to apply it appropriately in new situations.

COMPREHENSION
Comprehension consists of the abilities to translate, to interpret and to extrapolate information. It means that the student can go beyond the literal, to see the interrelationship between parts, and to make inferences about possible anticipated outcomes.

KNOWLEDGE
Knowledge refers to the ability to recall information. It represents the student's ability to draw on structures of stored information from his past, and to recognize those elements specific to the area being studied.

academic student. She seems able to incorporate most of Bloom's taxonomy of educational objectives and cognitive processes, and to engage the capacities of both her left and right hemispheres. However, she frequently talks about visual and auditory cognitive processes. Sometimes the cognitive processes are sequential and at other times they operate simultaneously. Kristin is left-handed.

You are asked to go over the transcripts carefully and to detect and identify those words and behaviors that help in understanding the cognitive processes operating within each student's head. After you have read the transcripts thoroughly, compare your writing format with those of the students. You might also ask yourself how you teach your students to write. Do your methods incorporate some of the cognitive processes and steps outlined by these two students?

Melissa's Learning Format

P = Psychologist
M = Melissa

P: Melissa, how do you go about writing a story? What do you do inside your head when you think about writing a story?

M: I make a picture (*moves eyes up and to the left*) and then I think about what words I can use to match my picture (*eyes move laterally to the left and then immediately down and to the left*).

P: Can you give me an example of how you make up a story?

M: Sure. I go . . . once upon a time (*eyes up and to the left*) there was a fish who lived under the sea, and (*eyes up and to the right*) people swim on top of the sea. Sometimes they go under the sea to catch fish in a bucket (*eyes up and to the left*). When they've caught a bucket of fish (*eyes up and to the right*), they swim back to land and then they fry the fish.

P: What else?

M: (*Eyes up to the left and then down to the left.*) And then there is seaweed (*eyes straight up*) under the sea for the fish to eat (*eyes up and to the left*). There are crabs, lobsters and sharks, but the sharks and whales are in the back. They're not in swimming pools or stuff (*eyes go down and to the left*). Especially, they don't go on land, because they like water. And (*eyes move up and to the right*) the sharks have a thing that sticks up, to beware of them. Sometimes (*eyes move down left*), the sharks go under the water to eat other fish. And then (*eyes up and left*) the whales come up, and sometimes they are friendly and eat stuff from your hand (*her eyes move straight ahead and then back up to the left*). Like, if you have a fish in your pot, how much would you feed it?

P: I don't know. How much?

M: You feed it about (*looks up and to the left*) a little scoop, a bit each day, so it would grow that big (*gestures with her hands*).

P: That's a good story. Excellent! How did you do that?

M: (*Eyes move up and to the left.*) I do a picture in my head, then I do words that match the picture of my fish story.

P: So, you take words that you hear yourself saying and match them to the story?

M: Yes.

P: Good. How do you know your story makes sense? That it is a good story?

M: (*Eyes move down and to the left and then down and to the right; her head tilt follows these movements.*) I read it. If (*eyes up to the left*) it doesn't make sense (*eyes move to the right*) I change it.

P: How do you know when to change it?

M: When it doesn't make sense.

P: How do you know when it doesn't make sense? (*Melissa's head tilts down and to the left, then her eyes move up and to the left.*) You said when you read it. So what about reading? It tells you that it doesn't go together? (*At this point, Melissa is looking laterally to the left and then she shifts her eyes up to her left.*)

M: If it doesn't go together, I just change it. Then I hand it to my teacher, and she tells me to make changes.

P: But, Melissa, how do you know it doesn't make sense? Do you read it out loud, or do you read it silently?

M: (*Eyes move up and left.*) I read it in my head!

P: So, when you're reading the story, something in your head lets you know that it isn't right. What happens?

M: (*Eyes move down and to the left.*) Like if it didn't have a capital . . . that's wrong (*eyes up and left*). Sometimes it doesn't make sense if it doesn't have a capital . . . like . . . (*moves eyes up and to the right*) Christmas tree sometimes doesn't make sense if it doesn't (*eyes down and to the left*) have a capital. (*Melissa pauses for a while and then moves her eyes up and to the left.*) It probably makes sense if you read it in your head and make a picture. If the picture didn't match the story (*eyes up and to the left*) then you'd have to change it (*eyes move up and to the right*).

P: All right. You say a sentence in your head and then try to make a picture in your head, to see if it fits or goes together? When you're reading the story to yourself you are making pictures of the story? (*Melissa looks up and to the right, moves her eyes down to the left and then back up to the left and nods.*) What happens if something's wrong with that picture? If it doesn't match the words, then the story isn't right?

M: I change the picture (*eyes move up and to the right*) in pencil. I usually write it out in pencil.

P: You change the story? You mean you change the sentences you wrote?

M: I change all the sentences! I erase all the sentences and then I . . . if my pictures don't match, I just change the sentences until they do.

Kristin's Strategy

P = Psychologist
K = Kristin

P: Kristin, you do really well in school. Is there a subject you think that you don't do well in?

K: No.

P: Let me ask you about writing stories. You are pretty good at writing stories and pretty good at writing poems, I hear. Is that right?

K: And book reports.

P: And book reports. I want you to tell me how you go about writing a story. Suppose the teacher gives you a topic. Suppose she says, "Kristin, I want you to write a story about computers." Tell me, what you would do inside your head in order to write that story?

K: I'd think about it, like make up some good things and put them together. (*Eyes move down and to the left.*)

P: You'll have to elaborate a little about that. When you say you think about it, what do you do inside your head? Do you make pictures? Talk to yourself? Have feelings? Just think about that now.

K: (*Kristin's eyes move down to the left, then straight up, then to the left and, finally down left again.*) I don't know.

P: Well, tell me a story about computers. Make it up for me.

K: OK. (*She looks up to the right and then down to the left.*) Once there was a computer named Bob, and (*eyes move up to the left*) he (*up to the right*) sat in a house (*eyes move down left, up right and up left*) and was never used (*down left*), so one day (*up left*) a girl came down and put a disc in it and the computer didn't know what to do (*looks straight ahead*). It just sat there and did nothing with its disc drive (*up left, up right*) and (*down left*) so the girl (*up left*) started hitting it. Bob then (*up left*) spat the disc out (*gestures, eyes down to the right*). She put it back in (*gestures*) and Bob spat it out again. He kept doing that for a couple of minutes (*head tilts left, and she looks up to the right*), so she got fed up and (*up right, up left*) Bob was left there for another ninety years.

P: Good. Now what I want to know is, how did you make up that story? How did you know to say all of those things?

K: I made a picture . . . sitting at the computer not knowing what to do, so it spat the disc out.

P: Now this is an interesting question, and I want you to think about it. When you were seeing the girl sitting at the computer desk, and the computer got mad at her and spat the disc out, did you sort of become part of the story? Did you become that little girl and feel what it would feel like to get mad at Bob?

K: (*Eyes up and to the left.*) No.

P: All right then. Were you looking at her doing that?

K: Yes. I only saw the back of the computer (*gestures with both hands*).

P: So you were looking at her from the back of the computer? You did not see the front?

K: I was looking at the computer from the back and I saw her face (*gestures, with facial grimaces*).

P: Oh, you mean like being at a movie, you were standing back and watching (*nods*). You didn't become the girl? You didn't see what the computer would look like through her eyes? (*Kristin shakes head, no.*) Well, why don't you go back there in that picture? (*Kristin moves her eyes straight up.*) You're looking from the back of the computer and you're watching her. Now, I want you to pretend that you can step into the picture, and step into her, and see what she sees and how she feels. Tell me what that would be like (*moves her eyes up to the left and then across to the right*). Describe it to me.

K: (*Looks straight up and moves back in the chair.*) Funny.

P: How is it funny?

K: (*Tilts head down to the right, but looks up to the left.*) Because the computer had a mean face on it!

P: And when you were sitting there, in her body, what did it feel like? What was she feeling?

K: I don't know.

P: OK., you know when she was hitting the computer? (*nods*) Step into her again and get in touch with what that feels like.

K: Can I close my eyes?

P: Sure.

K: (*Kristin closes her eyes, and then after a moment or two, opens them.*) Angry!

P: What was she doing? Show me what she was doing with her hands. (*Kristin demonstrates by using both fists as if she is hitting something.*) Was she hitting the computer?

K: Yes.

P: Did she hit it with her fists? (*nods*) So when you write stories . . . do you make pictures and then talk to yourself about the pictures? (*Kristin shakes her head, no.*) Then, what do you do?

K: I just see the picture (*eyes up right*) and then I write down what I think the picture is about.

P: When you write something down, do you say it to yourself first?

K: No.

P: So the words just come as you look at the pictures? (*nods head, yes*) Does that ever confuse you? It seems to me that the only time you hear what you write is when you write it down. (*nods*) How do you know it makes sense?

K: I read it after I'm finished.

P: And, as you read it, what happens? As you say the words to yourself, what happens on the inside?

K: I feel good that I've made a story (*gestures excitedly*)
P: So, if the story feels good to you, does that mean the ideas sort of flow along? (*nods*) So, as you read it do you also get pictures? (*nods*) It sounds as though you get more feelings than pictures, is that right? You know if the story is a good story by feelings?
K: (*Looks down left and then up to the left.*) I look at the pictures.
P: You know it's a good story by looking at the pictures inside your head? (*nods*) Do you see slides, like one picture after another one, or a movie?
K: (*Kristen looks straight ahead.*) Sort of like a movie (*defocuses and pupils dilate as she is answering*).
P: You see the movie running pretty . . .
K: But I don't see them moving . . . sometimes.
P: So you see stills, like slides? (*nods*)
K: Like my friend Audrey (*looks up to the right*). When we did a story with our group (*eyes up to the right*) at school (*up to the left*), she made some pictures and I remembered that and put it together. But I don't always make them move. If I want them to move, I make them move.
P: How do you make them move? How would you get them to move?
K: I think (*eyes up to the left*) about moving them.
P: Do you have a feeling attached to that? Or would you just say, hey pictures, move? What would you do?
K: (*Laughs*) I'd say, hey pictures, move! (*She looks up right and brings her hands together as if she is bringing the slides together.*)
P: I asked you if you knew whether or not the story was fluent . . . that means the ideas run smoothly . . . by looking at the pictures. What's the feeling telling you then? As you read your story, do you get good feelings?
K: Sometimes.
P: What do they tell you?
K: (*Looks down and to the left.*) It's a good story.

Both Melissa and Kristin exhibit component parts of Bloom's taxonomy and the underlying cognitive dynamics so evident in Andrea's creative writing strategy. When given a particular topic, each of them seems to rely on past learning experiences in terms of their writing. They access past memories of things they have seen or heard that are related to the topic at hand. They have the ability to use this knowledge base and reference structure to generate information on whatever topic presents itself. Hence, not only are they able to draw on past experiences, they are also able to comprehend the relationship among those experiences and the task at hand, as well as know how to adapt that knowledge to suit existing circumstances.

Each of them, to some extent, is able to blend the component parts into digestible "pictorial" chunks. Melissa, for example, creates images inside her head. Or, on occasion, she draws external representations of her story. Once she has developed these snapshots into a sequential arrangement, she finds words to fit the pictures, and uses those words as a basis for generating her stories. So, in order for Melissa to generate ideas for her stories, she employs a visual-sequential cognitive strategy. Once she has developed a series of "snapshots" or pictorial frames, she begins to associate words with her generated sequence of internal images. At this point, she is combining visual and verbal-auditory cognitive processes representative of the left and right hemispheres. Such an integrative process certainly suggests the beginnings of her synthesizing capacity.

Kristin, on the other hand, simply makes an internal picture or image of what she wants to write about. However, she does not appear to associate words with the internal pictures, although her accessing cues (eye movements, head tilts) suggest otherwise. Instead, she just writes the story. There is a possibility that, as she writes, she hears what she is writing and determines the appropriateness of the content. There is also a possibility that Kristin uses a visual digital strategy for writing her stories. She sees the written sentence in her head before writing it down on paper. That she feels excited when she reads the story, and knows it to be a good story, lends some support to the latter hypothesis.

Whereas Kristin reads her story aloud or internally and then employs internal criteria for determining its logical consistency, Melissa, at this stage of her development, relies on an external authority to judge her story's effectiveness. The use of an external reference or source of evaluation is somewhat normal at that age level.

This brief summary of the creative writing strategies used by Kristin and Melissa reveals some shared cognitive processes with Andrea's sophisticated writing format. There are similarities between the cognitive dynamics employed in all three creative writing strategies. Andrea's strategy, however, is representative of the higher cognitive functions (analysis, synthesis, evaluation) outlined in Bloom's taxonomy of cognitive processes and, at the same time, it is illustrative of the integrative processes of the left and right hemispheres.

Rationale for the Creative Writing Strategy

An effort was made to elicit the basic components or parts underlying the development of an effective creative writing strategy. At the same time, it was hypothesized that individuals would learn how to integrate the specialized functions of each cerebral hemisphere if they were able to externalize or internalize the structural components involved in an effective writing strategy. This was incorporated in the use of visual and auditory cognitive processes by using visual and

Figure 13

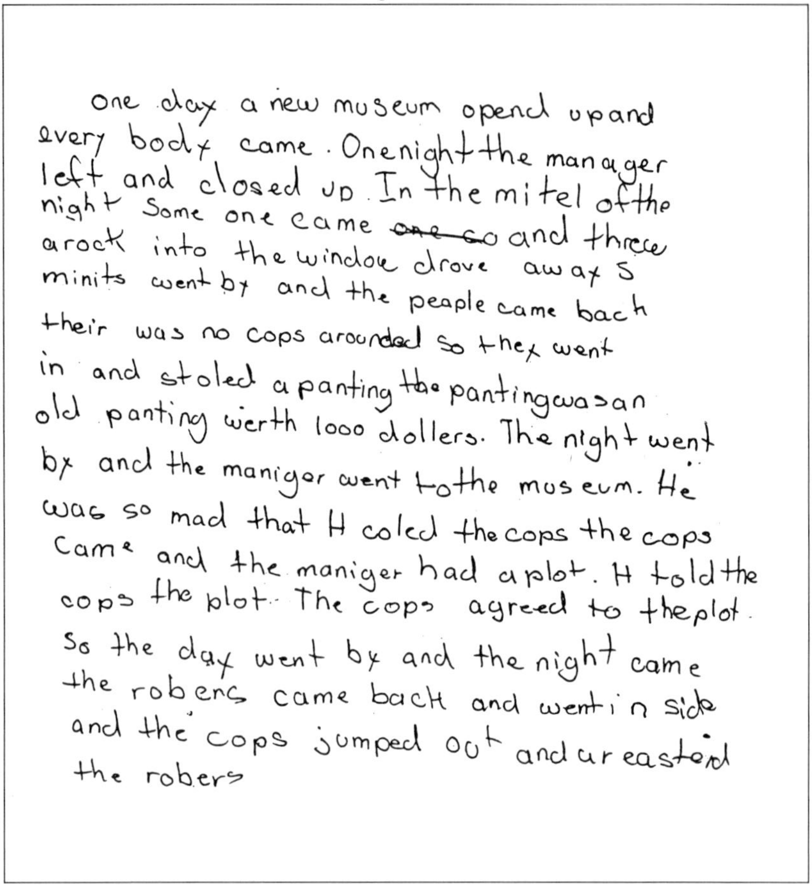

One day a new museum opend up and
every body came. One night the man ager
left and closed up. In the mitel of the
night Some one came one co and three
a rock into the window drove away 5
minits went by and the peaple came back
their was no cops aroonded so they went
in and stoled a panting the pantingwasan
old panting werth 1000 dollers. The night went
by and the manigor went to the museum. He
was so mad that H coled the cops the cops
Came and the maniger had a plot. H told the
cops the plot. The cops agreed to the plot.
So the day went by and the night came
the robers came back and went in side
and the cops jumped out and ur easterd
the robers

auditory cognitive modes and sequential and simultaneous cognitive processes. In this way, the creative writing procedure could address itself to students who prefer certain cognitive modalities, including the kinesthetic individual who organizes and stores information as "movement ideas". Such a student literally could be taught how to get a "feel" for a story; in effect, to become the characters and develop an experiential understanding of where the story is going, or the story's sequence of events.

The creative writing format was developed because many researchers detected language deficiencies in learning disabled students. The inability of these students to generate inner language, or to employ internal verbal mediation strategies as part of their thought processes, suggested a strategy that would rely on either a visual or kinesthetic mode. By relying on these two cognitive modalities, learning disabled students would be predisposed to generate ideas or concepts

Figure 14

One night a boy was staring at the stars
He saw the small dipper for the first time.
The boys name is Brian and he was ll.
He had dark drown hair and green eyes and
he was 4 fbot 10 intches.

Figure 14 (cont'd)

The next night Br♯n Went Back out side to
Look at the stars again.
Suddanly a (wish)of light went by him.He Jummped
up and went to see the thing that landed
He went and saw a huge ship^he ran away.

Figure 14 (cont'd)

He came back the next day and went to see
the ship exceped [sp] this time he brought his dad. [sp]
When they (reched) the ship it was gone. His
reached
dad said he was going back to the house.
Brain stayed there all night.
Suddenly it apeered. He jumped up this time.
appeared
He went and got this dad. It disaperd again.
poared
His dad left again.)

Figure 14 (cont'd)

He went back to the sip that hes dad
went to. when they got there every body
yelled oot Happy Birthday. the was so shool
Brain said "what about the sip?"
His dad said it was a big statue
that got talken away every time dcame.
Brain said "thanks to every one".

Figure 15

Once upon a time there lived a Prince who lived behind a stone wall. The prince owned a small house, a small pond and a speckled green frog. He was very lonely because the Prince could not find the girl of his dreams. But the prince had a negative attitude, he did not believe in miracle's

Figure 15 (cont'd)

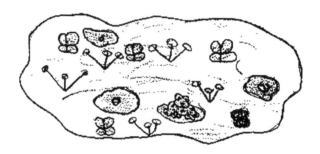

The miracle the Prince did not
believe in, was living right in his own
pond. It was the speckled green frog.
The frog was not really a frog, but a
princess who was put under a spell by
an evil wizard The frog princess knew
how to break the spell but she just
couldn't seem to break the spell because
she knew that never in a million year's
the prince would kiss her.
But then something happened.

Figure 15 (cont'd)

The prince was walking in his garden. He did not notice the frog at all, because he was feeling un-happy and a little bit worthless. He was feeling so bad, he felt he was worthless enough to kissa frag.

Figure 15 (cont'd)

The prince could not believe his
eye's! The frog just went poof,
Right in midair!
        and Right before his eye's
was a princess!. The could'nt
believe it!.

Figure 15 (cont'd)

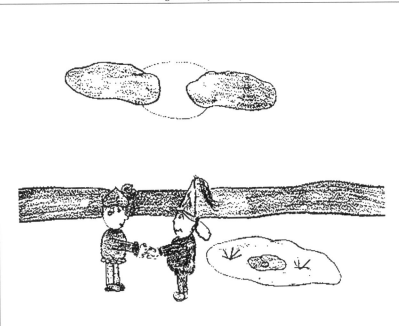

The prince was so happy,
out of happiness that he finally
found the woman of his dream's
he asked her to marry him, and
she said yes! Of course!

Figure 15 (cont'd)

So the prince and princess
were married
and moved to an open field with a
large castle, with a pond.
As any fairytale end's," They
lived happily ever after.

'THE END!"

based on one of their preferred cognitive systems. Using this method, they could generate the ideas first, and then use words to comment on the images or feelings. The visual pictures could be used as prompters or cues to conjure up words, verbal labels or vocabulary, that would not necessarily be available to them in any other way.

The creative writing procedure involves a variety of covert learning strategies such as brainstorming, analyzing, evaluating, without formally teaching them. This is somewhat akin to the strategy used by the wily Mr. Miyagi (The Karate Kid). While it appeared that Daniel was being conned into working (waxing the car, painting the fence, and so on), it was really a clever and covert demonstration of teaching the basics of karate without the apprentice being consciously aware of it.

The stories depicted in Figures 13, 14 and 15 are examples of what can be accomplished by teaching learning disabled students the creative writing format. They reflect pre-assessment levels of creative writing competencies, samples of the intervention phase, and final examples of the positive changes that had crystallized over a four-month remedial period. The stories were written by a Grade 4 female student, aged 10 years and four months.

As you examine the changes in the student's written work over the four-month period, you will notice variations in sentence structure; more logical consistency throughout her stories, better grasp of grammatical processes, and a radical change in her writing style. At first, she wrote in a tense, scribbly manner. But, as she persisted in learning the creative writing format, her handwriting seemed to become more fluid, reflective of a smoother thought pattern.

On the Wechsler Intelligence Scale for Children-Revised, (WISC - R) this student obtained a Full Scale IQ of 107 + /-6, a Verbal IQ of 90 and a Performance IQ of 128. This profile seems to be typical of many children who have difficulties/deficits in putting their thoughts on paper. Some researchers (Flaro, in preparation) conclude that such WISC - R patterns are positively correlated with deficiencies in internal speech and verbal mediation processes. Generally, the research indicates that these particular students do not talk to themselves; that is, they do not employ inner language or inner speech as part of their thought processes.

TABLE 6
The Creative Writing Format: Procedural Steps

Step 1.

First, select a topic.

Step 2.

The student is then asked to develop an internal or an external story (visual, auditory, kinesthetic, olfactory, gustatory) based on all his or her past experiences and knowledge associated with this topic. By having the student think about past activities, people, places, things seen or read about, information heard or experienced, the student should be able to develop a general picture: a composite of all the knowledge he has available about the topic. This information can best be gathered either by creating an internal image or picture that would include all that he knows, or by drawing an external picture representative of the content of the topic picture.

Step 3.

The student may use only those pieces of information pertinent to the task. To do this he will need to select from his composite picture, the knowledge and bits and pieces of information having a significant connection to the topic. This "chunking down" process, to become even more specific, requires the student to ask himself questions about the setting, characters and sequence of the story. However, for many students, this procedure will be too difficult, so the teacher needs to instruct the student in the use of the who, what, where, when, why and how questions. By using these questions, the gathered information will automatically chunk down into a more manageable size.

Step 4.

With the information collected through brainstorming and self-questioning techniques, the student is asked to make an internal image or picture (the first slide) of the starting point of the story. This is the beginning frame of a potential movie. The picture, or frame, however, should be a still shot, like the first slide of a cartoon story or movie. The reason for this first slide is to enable some students to draw the slide, rather than imagine it.

Step 5.

Next, the student develops the content of the first slide as fully as possible. With that slide completed, he then creates a picture, or slide, which is the ending or conclusion of the story. He now knows how the story will begin and how it will end.

Step 6.

With a beginning and an ending to his story, the student must now fill in the space between these two slides. To complete this segment of the procedure, he can use the information he has gathered in previous steps to assist him in completing the story sequence. He can do this by either working forward from the beginning to end of his story, or by working backward from end to beginning. He would, in any case, begin to develop internal or external pictures that would bridge the pictures sequentially from end to end.

The student must now evaluate whether the pictures do, in fact, connect sequentially and temporally to each other. A trial run can be used to determine the effectiveness of the images and, consequentially, the logical consistency of the story. The student can pretend that he is watching the slides develop into a movie. Does the movie flow smoothly? If it does, the student can assume the story has some logical internal consistency and is sufficiently well organized to pass muster. If it does not, then more slides may need to be interpolated between those that seem disconnected.

Step 7.
Now the student is to look closely at each slide or picture and verbally brainstorm words to describe it. This procedure is similar to clustering or webbing. The student brainstorms as many words as possible that describe the contents of the slide. Once he has completed one slide or picture, he moves on to the next, until all slides or images have a list of brainstormed words underneath them that verbally describe the story to be. The student will incorporate these words into his main story.

Step 8.
Once the student has mastered the above steps, he writes a story about each slide, in a sequential manner. That is to say, the student looks at the internal or external picture of the first slide and writes as much as possible about the content of that slide. He is to describe the slide in terms of the characters, what they are doing, where the event takes place, and how the action started. For the student to learn to generate these ideas, he may need to employ transition words (BECAUSE, FURTHERMORE, THEN, NEXT, THEREFORE, BUT) to assist in the writing process. The student continues the process by writing as much as possible about each slide—what he sees, hears, feels, smells, and tastes—until all slides are completed.

Step 9.
Having finished the written work, the student is now ready to evaluate the effectiveness and cohesiveness of his completed story. He can do this by reading the story out loud, or by subvocalizing and watching the internal pictures as he talks. In this way, the student will be able to see, feel or hear whether the story flows smoothly, one slide connecting with the next in a logical order.

To assess the merits and effectiveness of his story, the student may need to employ some internal evaluative criteria that let him know if the story is developing credibly. He may, for example, experience an internal twinge that signals to him that the story doesn't flow at a particular point, or that it doesn't follow from one slide to the next. Some students may become aware that whenever the fluency of the story is in doubt, or the slides do not connect smoothly one to another in a logical sequence, they see their internal pictures become fuzzy and out of focus. This visual experience will alert the student that the sequence of the story is not connected at the point(s) where the slide(s) begin to fade or lose focus. As he listens to the progression of the story, he may feel that it doesn't sound right. He can stop at this point and work on the poorly written part of his script until he is satisfied.

Step 10.

Some students may have difficulty in generating clear, focused, internal images. It is more than appropriate to have those students draw pictures of the story sequences. The procedure could be facilitated and reinforced by having the student write stories about pictures provided by the teacher. In fact, the teacher could have the student look at a picture, brainstorm verbal descriptions of its contents, and then write as much as possible about it. The student could also be taught the kinds of questions to use to elicit information about sequence, cohesiveness and order. The teacher could also encourage the use of transition words to generate more ideas and to improve the flow of the story.

For the kinesthetic learner and processor, the teacher may want the student to look at a particular picture and then act it out, or the teacher could have other students act it out. As the students are role playing, the teacher can ask questions about a particular character, what that character sees around him, how that character feels about being in the story, and what other characters in the story are like.

Once the students have acted out the story, others will have a personal reference for it and can then write about what they saw, heard, felt, smelled or tasted. The purpose of this exercise is to have the external process eventually become internalized so that each student can automatically develop and use this cognitive strategy. As well, each student will use his own personal history and past experiential learning to create individualistic and unique stories.

Figure 16

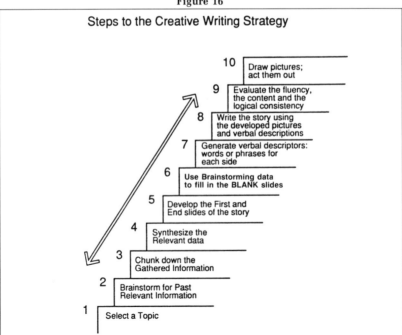

Steps to the Creative Writing Strategy

10 — Draw pictures; act them out

9 — Evaluate the fluency, the content and the logical consistency

8 — Write the story using the developed pictures and verbal descriptions

7 — Generate verbal descriptors: words or phrases for each side

6 — Use Brainstorming data to fill in the BLANK slides

5 — Develop the First and End slides of the story

4 — Synthesize the Relevant data

3 — Chunk down the Gathered Information

2 — Brainstorm for Past Relevant Information

1 — Select a Topic

Suggested Exercises for Parents and Teachers

The teacher or parent needs to look for, and carefully study the regularities in the learner's behavior. Behavioral regularities can range from eye movements to head tilts, or to adjusting body posture as a means of accessing particular cognitive systems or differential modes of mental processing. External behavioral responses appear to be correlated to the learner's habits of cognition. To be able to use the proposed model in this chapter, you will need to develop your sensory acuity and observational skills to a level that will enable you to map the behavioral and cognitive strategies the student employs to think, to spell, problem solve, read, answer questions and/or do arithmetic. Each subject area will elicit a different set of behavioral and cognitive strategies that can be mapped out to understand the internal mental processes and sequence, or simultaneous use, of representational cognitive systems responsible for effective or inefficient learning.

It is useful to think of the individual student as being composed of three interrelated systems: External Behavior, Internal Response and Internal Processing. In this way, you can begin to understand that no external behavior occurs without being associated with some internal physiological response or to some internal processing system. Thus, the direct observation of external behavioral patterns (i.e., eye movements) will provide important information about the internal structure of the student's thought processes. Once you have detected and identified a recurrent set of behavioral responses, you can then use verbal questioning to determine how the observed external behaviors are related to internal processing systems. In this way, you will gain information about the learner's internal cognitive systems as well as learn to develop highly refined sensory acuity and perceptual recognition programs. You will also learn how lateralized behavioral response is associated with hemispheric styles for processing information.

Figure 17

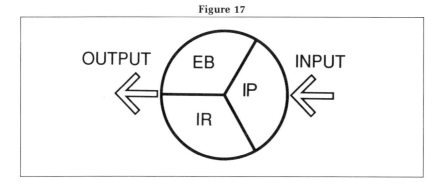

The teacher and parent must also be able to use sensory-specific words in gathering information about the mental processes the learner is using to think and learn. Your verbal questioning must incorporate these sensory-specific words as part of your response repertoire. Instead of saying, "How do you think?" or, "What do you do inside your head when you spell a word?", you incorporate words that give the student more information about his internal processes: ''Do you make internal pictures?'' or, ''Do you talk to yourself, or attempt to sound out the words?'' This skill is also very important when students are given specific verbal instructions on how to carry out an assignment. The more specific you can be, the greater the probability of the student responding in an appropriate way.

Exercise One

Your first task in this exercise is simply to observe and chart a student's eye-movement patterns as he works in various subject areas. Whenever the student spells, note which external eye movement patterns are used to obtain correct answers as opposed to incorrect responses. Does the learner use the same eye-movement patterns for mathematics, spelling, oral answers, problem solving and reading comprehension? How does the learning disabled student compare in eye-movement patterns with your regular classroom student? Does the learning disabled student prefer a certain set of eye-movement patterns, such as consistently accessing up and right? What do these eye-movement patterns mean in terms of internal processing systems and hemispheric information processing styles?

The eye-movement charts on the next page are provided to give you some direction of how to map cognitive systems based on external behaviors. You need to know that some eye movements will be difficult to detect, especially in truly gifted students, since they seem to have quick access to stored information. When, however, they do not immediately produce the information they seek, you will observe eye movements in all directions as they internally search for an answer in all representational systems. It is important to realize that the direction of eye movements will reflect the learner's cognitive and hemispheric styles, depending on the lateralization of eye gaze. Please be willing to experiment, have fun, and gather information through questioning.*

Exercise Two

This exercise requires the fine-tuning of your observational skills, in the sense that you will begin to label the eye movements according to the eye-movement chart presented in Chapter 2. To refresh your memory, let's discuss what eye-movement behavior means in a normally organized right-handed child. The student who looks up to his left is accessing eidetic imagery; that is, he is recalling past visual information that seems associated with long-term visual memory (Vr). Looking up to the right indicates visual reconstruction; that is, he is constructing imagery that he hasn't seen before. This eye movement seems associated with visual-sequential cognitive processes and reflects left hemispheric processing. It also seems correlated with short-term visual memory (Vc). Lateral eye movements to the left indicate auditory recall (Ar) and seem linked to auditory memory. These eye movements seem to reflect nonverbal auditory processes such as jingles, nursery rhymes and intonation patterns. Right lateral eye movements corresponds to auditory construction processes; that is, they are indicative of putting your thoughts into words, such as when you are to present a workshop for the first time. You would, in fact, verbally rehearse what you were going to say to the audience. When the student looks down and to his left, he is

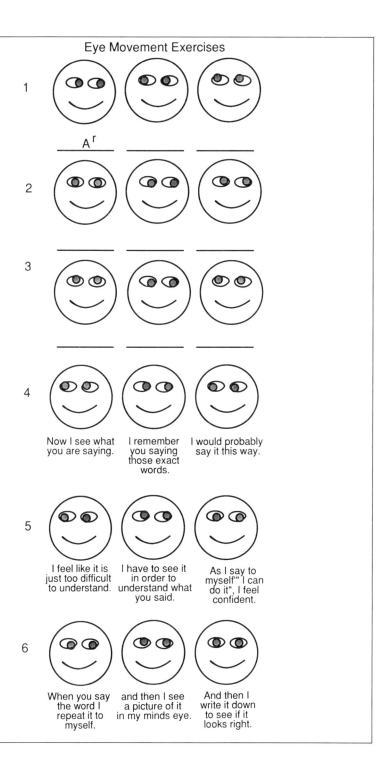

Eye Movement Exercises

engaging in internal dialogue; he is having an internal conversation with himself. This eye movement represents the use of verbal-mediation strategies, such as sounding out the word. Eye-movement behavior down and to the right signifies internal visceral/kinesthetic feelings. That type of eye movement is often seen in learning disabled children who find learning quite difficult. Often, they will look down and to the right, feel negatively associated internal responses, and say, ''I don't know.'' Some research that I am presently doing suggests that such a behavior pattern is also related to the student's belief systems, and that his external behavior becomes shaped or nominalized to support and to reinforce these belief systems. Some children look straight ahead, dilate their pupils, and seem to be off in a world of their own. This eye-movement pattern indicates the use of visualization processes, with the picture or image being externalized to the individual. This means that the student sees the picture as though outside himself. Constricted pupils can be representative of either auditory or kinesthetic cognitive processes. Students who look straight up seem to be activating visual-motor processes; that is, they are seeing themselves write something. A motoric response is associated with the internal picture; a type of synesthesia pattern. This internal representation occurs as a result of an actual external visual-motor pattern.

Some research indicates that the eye-movement patterns in left-handed individuals may be totally reversed. According to research, this would apply to approximately five percent of the population of left-handed individuals. For the other 95 percent, the eye-movement patterns seem to be reversed in one or, at most, two quadrants. My oldest daughter, eleven-year-old Kristin, is left-handed and accesses up to the right to recall pictures of past words. Her eidetic imagery seems stored up and to the right. Whenever asked to spell a word, she immediately looks up and to the right and sees the whole word. She says the word to herself and sees pictures of the syllabic units that correspond to her phonemic analysis. It is interesting to note that Kristin hardly ever uses phonemic analysis to spell words. Please use the drawing below to refresh your memory about eye movements.

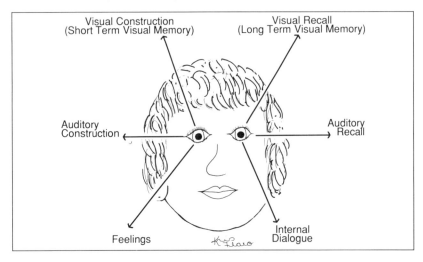

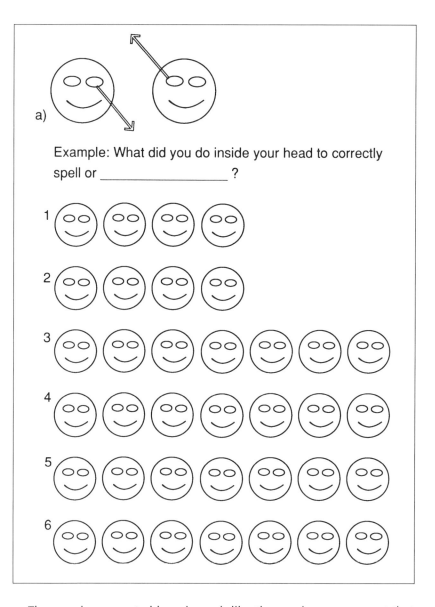

The exercise presented here is much like the previous one except that you have to label the eye movement with the appropriate verbal symbols. This exercise also requires you to ask questions so that you can make your own judgments about the usefulness of eye movements and how they seem correlated to internal processing systems. Again, have students spell orally or do mathematics orally while you chart their eye-movement patterns with the appropriate symbol. As you progress in developing the ability to detect and to identify eye-movement patterns, compare the behavioral strategies the students use for various subjects. When you ask a student to define a word in, say, science, is his strategy different from the one he uses for mathematics? What does he do differently inside his head? Is he in fact aware of what is going on in his mind? Does he prefer only one system, which may be related to a single eye movement, or does he use more than one cognitive system, as does my daughter Kristin? As an added adventure, ask children how they think about things. My younger daughter Melissa, when asked this question, placed her hands under her chin and rested her elbows on the table. Looking straight up, she said: "Oh, I just don't know. I sometimes see pictures in my mind, such as the word PARK." Melissa is very good at spelling and uses almost the same eye-movement pattern when doing her basics. She is also very good at mathematics; in fact, this is her strong point at the present. As you can see, you can gather a lot of information about a child's internal processing systems, based on eye-movement patterns alone. So, experiment and amuse yourself. The exercises below are for your learning experience and interest.

The detection and identification of regularities in human behavior are important observation skills that can be used to elicit specific cognitive and learning strategies that many students automatically and unconsciously employ to achieve academically in the school environment. They can also be generalized to sports or other athletic activities (Loehr, J.E., 1982; Garfield, C.A., 1984). When we develop a particular behavioral or cognitive strategy for doing something well, we seem reluctant to give it up, even in the face of obvious negative feedback. Learning disabled students are no different in the sense that, once they find a particular learning strategy or cognitive format that achieves the outcome they want, they continue to employ it, even in inappropriate contexts. In a sense, it's like playing the one-armed bandit; as soon as you win, even once, you continue to play, because you know you will eventually win again. Unfortunately, these machines do not work according to this rule or expectation. When we do not win, like learning disabled children we become upset and complain that the machines are fixed, or else we kick the machine to show it how stupid it is. The learning disabled student finds similar ways to rationalize his inability to solve a particular problem, write a specific story, spell some words, or to complete a math computation. It is his way of dealing with frustration. The learning disabled student may act aggressively, refuse to do any work, or may disrupt the classroom in order to get out of a situation that defines his self-worth in negative terms.

The foregoing exercise was designed to teach you specific observational skills for gathering information. It was based on detecting minimal cues made manifest by the learning disabled student so that you could learn to tie external behavioral responses with internal mental processes. Other minimal cues mentioned throughout this chapter are also important in the detection and identification of external behavioral strategies and internal cognitive formats. Some of these minimal behavioral cues are: head tilts or head orientations; pupillary changes; physiological shifts; gestures; hand movements; muscle tonus changes; facial coloration changes; eye blinks; body postures; voice quality changes: tempo, pitch, volume, timbre; and breathing pattern shifts: rate, location, depth. While it is not expected that you learn to be sensitive to all these minimal cues, it is important that you become consciously aware of what they mean in terms of internal mental processes. For example, can you tell, on the basis of body language. what preferred cognitive representational system the student will use in his thought processes? When a student speaks in a rapid, high-pitched-voice, what internal mental process do you associate with this? Is he having feelings? Talking to himself? Processing information sequentially, simultaneously or integratively? What about the student who talks in a slow, hesitant voice pattern (the movie star, James Stewart, comes readily to mind)? How are breathing patterns related to internal representational systems? How do different breathing patterns affect the reading process or influence one's reading comprehension? How does moving one's head rather than one's eyes affect reading rate or reading comprehension? Is there a particularly good posture for reading and comprehension? What is it? How do exceptionally good readers posture themselves? How are they breathing? What are they doing on the inside? What would happen to an learning disabled student's reading ability if you taught him how to assume this same posture: to breathe as good readers do, to read using the same internal mental processes? These are some important issues that you need to understand in order to help learning disabled children to learn in different ways; to teach them to think differently; to develop the cognitive flexibility to approach problems from all perspectives, and to be able to learn to how learn!

Exercise Three

As a more complex exercise for the truly interested, and those individuals who like challenges, take the time to observe the relationship between cognitive representational systems and:

a. head tilts
b. breathing patterns
c. facial coloration
d. volume, tempo
e. eye blinks
f. hand gestures
g. body types
h. postural shifts
i. eyebrow movement
j. folded arms
k. the telephone posture

The second part of this exercise requires you to create certain internal experiences and, one by one, change the above behaviors and notice how this affects your internal representations. For example, read in your normal way then change your posture so that you are slouched over, looking down. Does this change of posture affect the way you read and, if so, in what way? Next, lie on the floor on your stomach and read for a little while. Now turn over onto your back and read some more. Is there a difference between how you read in one position as opposed to the other? Pretend that you are a student in class who reads by slouching over his desk, supporting his head on his forearms. How does this affect your ability to read and comprehend?

Take as much time as needed to create a clear and vivid internal experience. Once you have it, shift your breathing pattern to either abdominal breathing, diaphragmatic breathing or upper chest breathing, and notice what happens to your internal representation. Does it change? What specifically changes? Now try to complete some mental mathematical computations, such as 17 times 17, inside your head and shift your breathing patterns, eye movements or head tilts. Notice what happens to your internal processing systems. Do you lose the picture? Are you forced to rely on your fingers? Do you become upset because you can't see the picture anymore?

It is important that you do these exercises, so that you can learn how external behaviors do affect internal processing strategies. How you breathe, where you look, or how you talk, can have a profound impact on your cognitive processes. Ask learning disabled children some of these questions and have them do the above exercises and you will learn some important things. As an adjunct to this, we know that some children are future-oriented; that is, they spend their time in class thinking about things that are going to happen on the weekend, or which TV program to watch, and so on. Other students are present-focused. They seem to respond impulsively, to the moment, without any thought of negative consequences or behavioral outcomes. Still others are past-oriented and seem to be replaying old videotapes inside their heads.

Can you figure out what external behaviors go along with each time frame? What evidence can you use to detect and identify time frames in students? Who's the historian? The futurist? The here and now gestaltist? This exercise requires a high level of sophistication, so if you manage to do it, please pat yourself on the back, you deserve it! Time frames are important in the area of creating, writing, projecting and remembering, so it might be useful to recognize the student who can do these things, and to detect the skills used, so that you can teach these same skills to the other children in your class — especially those who are having some learning difficulties.

CHAPTER 5

CONQUERING READING COMPREHENSION AND MATHEMATICS LEARNING DISABILITIES THROUGH COGNITIVE ABILITY PATTERNING

 EADING COMPREHENSION
A number of investigators have proposed a variety of factors as potential causes of reading comprehension deficits (Bayliss & Livesay, 1985; Bettelheim & Zelan, 1982; Das, Kirby & Jarman, 1979; Haber & Haber, 1981; Nagel, 1985; Rampp, 1980; Ross, 1976; Samuels & Esienberg, 1981; Wittrock, 1981). Generally, these include poor attentional processes, lack of meaningful interpretations and connections to the written words, the deployment of inappropriate information processing strategies, poor decoding skills, deficits in visual/auditory perception, and a host of others.

That there should be so many factors cited as possible contributing causes of reading comprehension deficits is hardly surprising, given the lack of a precise definition of the reading process among researchers (Carroll, 1972; Golinkoff, 1975/76; Spiro, Bruce & Brewer, 1980). Since there is no consensus on the definition of reading comprehension, this would presuppose that there are a number of cognitive processes involved in the task of decoding and understanding the written word. This is aptly demonstrated in Irwin's (1986:9) definition of reading comprehension:

> Comprehension can be seen as the process of using one's prior experiences (reader context) and the writer's cues (text context) to infer the author's intended meaning. This process can involve understanding and selectively recalling ideas in individual sentences (microprocesses), inferring relationships between clauses and/or sentences (integrative processes), organizing ideas around summarizing ideas (macroprocesses), and making inferences not necessarily intended by the author (elaborative processes). These processes work together (interactive processes)

and can be controlled and adjusted by the reader as required by the reader's goals (metacognitive processes) and the total situation in which comprehension is taking place (situational context).

While this definition offers a wealth of information about the types of covert cognitive processes involved in the reading comprehension act, it does not do much for the educator's reading comprehension level! The Reading Comprehension Format (Table 7) proposed in this section is based on Wittrock's (1981) generative processing model: the research on cognitive and metacognitive processes; visual imagery and verbal mediation strategies; the neurolinguistic paradigm, and the cerebral specialization model.

In Wittrock's generative processing model, it is suggested that for the student to comprehend what is being read, he must be able to extract meaning from the written words. In fact, the student must actively participate in the construction of meaningful associations and connections with his own personal history of experiences, learnings and previously acquired knowledge. This ability to transform written text into meaningful understanding requires the employment of imaginal cognitive operations and verbal mediation strategies. This active cognitive, constructive process provides the reader with the appropriate psychological mechanisms and meaningful associations required to form a sound basis for comprehending and understanding written text.

The overall purpose of the generative processing model can best be illustrated by quoting Flaro (1987/88) at some length:

> In most academic settings, students are taught to read with the sole purpose being to reproduce the information on examinations. They do not learn to relate the learned information to past experiences or learnings, nor do they learn how to organize it into useful and coherent schemata and more meaningful mental representations. This process prevents students from learning to generalize the information to other academic contexts and to apply what they have learned in a meaningful way (Samuels & Eisenberg, 1981; Vellutino & Scanlon, 1982). On the other hand, the generative processing model involves the cognitive interactions between the reader's knowledge and experiences, the context and the text itself. It is designed to develop optimal transfer of learning and, (at the same time), to provide the reader with a basis for making meaningful associations and connections to the written material (Gordon & Poze, 1979).

The information processing model hypothesizes that the differences in reading comprehension ability may be the logical by-products of the type of internal cognitive strategy being employed by the student.

Generally, this model suggests that when information processing systems are incompatible with instructional demands, deficits in performance are likely to occur. More specifically, a number of investigators have proposed that reading comprehension requires the integration of sequential and simultaneous cognitive processes (Bayliss & Livesay, 1985; Brailsford, Snart & Das, 1984; Das, Snart & Mulcahy, 1982; Leong, 1982).

Similarly, the cerebral specialization model emphasizes the integration of right-brain and left-brain cognitive processes as a necessary requirement for the development of effective comprehension strategies. While the left hemisphere specializes in analyzing and breaking down large information units into smaller cognitive chunks, such as in associating sounds with individual letters, the right hemisphere is predisposed to the synthesizing of smaller units into whole chunks. Both styles of processing information are important for developing the skills involved in reading comprehension.

The neurolinguistic paradigm attempts to identify the number of cognitive systems involved epistemologically in thinking. This model has been discussed in previous sections and will not be further elaborated upon here. However, the reader should recall Myklebust's discussion of intrasensory, interneurosensory and integrative neurosensory learning processes involved in the development of spelling, reading, mathematics, and reading comprehension.

The following case histories illustrate some of the elements that can interfere with the overall development of reading comprehension. These transcripts, based on audio cassette recordings and clinical notes, provide the reader with examples of what cognitive processes are actively involved in the ability to comprehend the written word. By employing a think aloud format or, more technically, a "protocol analysis" procedure, we begin to gain some important insight into how students' minds work; we begin to ferret out the cognitive modalities and mental modes of processing that seem to be prerequisite abilities for the development of effective reading comprehension processes.

Larry: A Case History

Larry was a Grade 3 student, aged eight years and five months. He was referred by his classroom teacher who had attended one of my workshops. The initial complaint by Larry's mother was that her son did not comprehend what he was reading. However, if someone else read to him he had no difficulty understanding what was read. The teacher's report indicated similar findings.

Previous intellectual assessment revealed that Larry was of average intelligence, with no particular patterns of weakness, and he had an exceptional strength in auditory short-term memory. What follows is the initial information gathering assessment with Mrs. B. and her son, Larry.

P = Psychologist
B = Mrs. B.
L = Larry

P: Mrs. B., tell me a little about what you perceive Larry's problem to be.
B: Well, Larry has trouble comprehending what he reads. He's a slow reader, and this may be causing the problem. Yet, when the teacher or I read to him he understands really well. He's been tested, but no one seems to be able to determine what the problem is.
P: So, you are saying that Larry can comprehend a story if it is read to him?
B: Yes. But when he reads it to himself, he does not remember what the story was about, nor does he understand the content.
P: Larry, I want you to read this book for me.
    [As Larry read the story out loud, I noted that he appeared to be a one-word reader: he didn't read fluently, or with emphasis, but in a consistent monotone, holding the book in his lap as he read. Acting on intuition, I asked him to hold the book up, slightly above eye level, and to go on reading. As he continued to read, there was a considerable difference in his delivery. This time, his reading was fluent and now there was emphasis placed on the words. Why? I asked him to place the book on his lap again and to continue with the story. Larry did so, and immediately reverted to his previous one-word pattern, with much hesitation and labored breathing.]
B: I can't believe the difference in his reading when he holds his book down there and then reads with it up above. What's going on?
P: I don't know. Larry, tell me what you just read. (*Larry searches for the information, but does not produce a satisfactory answer. It's as if he's spending so much time decoding the words, sounding out each syllable, that he has no time to make meaningful associations with the written words.*) All right, Larry. Let me read some of this story and then you can tell me about it.
    [I then read two pages of the story, and while reading I noticed that Larry's eyes moved upward in response to the read material. I continued to read, gathering information about Larry's external behaviors and what cognitive modalities he may be using to understand and comprehend the read material. After two pages, I stopped reading to ask Larry some questions about what he has heard.]

P: Larry, what was the story about? (*Larry's eyes move upward as he gives me an accurate description of the story.*)

[At the end of this session, I asked Larry some specific questions about the story, one of which was: Why was the dinosaur hiding? Larry responded to my questions by looking up and answering them all correctly.]

P: Larry, what were you doing in your head while I was reading the story to you?

L: I was thinking about what you were saying and trying to see it.

P: You mean that you were making pictures of the characters and the dinosaur?

L: Yes, I tried to see the actors as if I was watching a movie on my TV, or at a show.

P: So, when you listen to someone else read a story you can sit back and make internal pictures of the story. When someone asks you questions about it you kind of look up and see the story with your mind's eye? (*I point upward to where Larry was looking as he was reading the story.*)

L: Yes, that's what I do.

P: What happens when you read a story silently to yourself? Do you make pictures then?

L: (*Larry thinks about this for some time.*) No, I'm too busy sounding out the words.

P: When you read to yourself, you don't make pictures or images in your head, you just repeat the words to yourself as you sound them out. This must mean that you are so busy saying the words that you don't have time for constructing images?

L: Well, I find it hard to read and make pictures in my head at the same time.

There followed some discussion with Mrs. B. regarding what had been deduced from Larry's reading, and I explained to her the significance of what had been learned about his reading habits. I then spent some time teaching Larry how to read a sentence, stop, look up, and make a mental picture of what he had just read. He was to do this, one sentence at a time, until he fully understood the process. He was to proceed to two or three sentences, and then to paragraphs, until he could read and generate images simultaneously.

Mrs. B. was given the task of teaching Larry to respond more efficiently to whole words, rather than sound them out. She was asked to construct some cards of whole words and then to tachistoscopically flash them at Larry, giving him only a few seconds to respond before proceeding to the next word. This task was to develop his recognition span as well as to interrupt his phonetic habit of sounding out every word. Mrs. B. was to work with Larry every night until the strategies became automatic. Similarly, the teacher was told what I had determined was the possible cause of Larry's difficulties, and asked to pursue my recommendations within the classroom. In this way, the new learning strategies would become naturally generalized to the classroom.

I saw Larry several more times, and gave his mother help in refining her remedial procedures and assisting Larry in developing more effective learning formats. Follow-up after three months revealed that he was doing exceptionally well in reading comprehension. In fact, the results of the year end's *Canadian Tests of Basic Skills* indicated a two to three year jump in reading comprehension over an eight-month period. [It must be remembered that both the mother and the teacher, as well as the resource room specialist, worked consistently with Larry on a regular basis. They employed the recommendations offered and faithfully worked at developing the cognitive strategies. Larry's success occurred because of their dedication and his own desire to learn.]

Analysis of this brief case study reveals that Larry can comprehend what is read to him, but, when reading silently, he invests so much energy in decoding words that he is unable to make the meaningful associations so necessary for comprehension to occur. In fact, the practice of decoding words prevented Larry from drawing on his past knowledge and experiential resources in order to translate the text symbols into some meaningful representation.

Observations of external behaviors and questions about the cognitive processes involved in both situations produced some interesting findings. The contrastive approach revealed some major differences in terms of the cognitive processes operating under different circumstances. While listening to someone else vocalize a story, Larry was able to generate internal imagery based on past knowledge and information and consequently form the associations necessary for his comprehension ability. However, in silent reading his attention processes were so focused on decoding skills that he could not employ his imaginal abilities to comprehend the content of the story.

With the knowledge gathered in this diagnostic interview, tentative hypotheses could be generated about the nature of Larry's comprehension deficits; mainly lack of use of positive resources. His inability to apply his inner resources under these circumstances contributed significantly to his problems. As a result of these hypotheses two tentative interventions were formulated:

1) Teach him to respond more globally and automatically to words. This would increase his recognition span and at the same time force him to interrupt his old decoding strategy.

2) By having him read a sentence and then stop, look up and generate an internal image, he would naturally be employing an effective

strategy that he already used when someone else read the story. Only in this situation he would be contextualizing an already efficient reading comprehension strategy.

The follow-up indicated that the new strategies were working very well, producing the desired results. The effectiveness of these brief strategic interventions was so pronounced that no further remedial treatment was deemed necessary for Larry.

Corinne: A Case History

This case history deals with a Grade 5 student called Corinne who had better than average intelligence but who seemed to be unable to read a story with any degree of comprehension. This case history has, for the most part, been constructed from clinical notes and poorly taped audio cassette material.

Mr. W., at the initial interview, presented the psychologist with an accumulation of psycho-educational tests that had been administered to his daughter Corinne. He explained that the "testing professionals" had not been able to determine the causative agent responsible for her inability to read with any degree of understanding and comprehension. Furthermore, Mr. W. stated categorically that there was something definitely wrong with his daughter; that when she read she did so in a very slowly and laboriously. She seemed very anxious when she had to read and did not appear to grasp the meaning of the words in the text.

Yet, at home she could read very well to a younger sibling, aged four years. Both parents had heard her read quite well to the younger child but noticed that her reading fluency dropped dramatically once they appeared on the scene. Consequently, they began to assume that they had somehow taught her to hate reading and that perhaps they were just expecting too much of Corinne. They firmly believed that she had the capability and intelligence to become a good reader. They knew from previous discussions with her that she was very intelligent. She appeared to have a good vocabulary and to be able to articulate her thoughts in a logically appropriate manner.

I saw Corinne alone for one session, to create a safe and secure environment for her to discuss her difficulties. At the same time, information about her special interests, hobbies and favorite television programs was gathered from Mr. W. and used throughout the session to develop the degree of rapport that would be necessary to elicit the appropriate information about the cognitive dynamics contributing to her difficulties. When this rapport was established, I asked Corinne to consider the possibility of learning some new procedures that would assist her in developing reading comprehension. After some discussion, she agreed to see me again, when we would work on developing more effective strategies to improve her reading comprehension ability.

P = Psychologist
W = Mr. W.
C = Corinne

P: Mr. W., Corinne and I have talked about some of her difficulties relative to her poor reading comprehension. She does not know why she is unable to understand what she reads, but describes it as losing track of where she is at and not knowing what she has read. We also discovered that she has better comprehension when engaged in silent reading; however, when she is asked to read aloud her reading comprehension decreases dramatically. This session is designed to explore some of these findings. Do you have any questions?

W: No, I would just like to be able to help Corinne read more effectively, but I don't know how to do this.

P: Corinne, I'm going to ask you to read something silently to yourself. I know this will be difficult for you, but in order to help you I need to gather some more information. Is this all right?

C: Yes (*said softly as she looks down and to the right*).

[I gave Corinne a book to read and watched her external behavioral responses to this task. As she began to read, I noticed frequent swallowing, erratic breathing and signs of increased heartbeat. After several minutes, I stopped Corinne and questioned her on what she had read.]

P: Corinne, what happened as you began to read that story? What was happening on the inside? Were you making pictures, talking to yourself, or having lots of feelings?

C: I was having lots of feelings.

P: What kind of feeling were they? Were they good feelings or bad feelings? Did you feel happy, scared or frightened? Or, did you feel anxious, kind of nervous?

C: I felt nervous and scared.

P: When you experienced these feelings, what happened as you read the words?

C: (*She looks down and to the right.*) I don't know. I just felt so anxious that I couldn't see what I was reading.

P: Do you mean that the words weren't clear, or that you had a hard time understanding what you read?

C: (*Takes a deep breath and looks down right.*) No, it was almost like the letters disappeared and I couldn't see them. They sort of got fuzzy . . . I don't know how to explain it.

P: That's all right, you are doing really well. Let's try another experiment. Here is the story, where you left off. I want you to read it again, but this time I want you to read it out loud to me. (*At this request, Corinne's heart began to pound, her face became extremely tense and she visibly paled. Her breathing became erratic and her hands began to tremble noticeably.*) All right, stop. What happened here? You looked really nervous and anxious. What was going on inside you?

C: (*As she spoke, the author could still detect the nervousness in her voice. She also appeared to have quite a bit of difficulty articulating her thoughts.*) I . . . felt really nervous. My heart beat faster and my hands began to shake. I don't know why.

P: Corinne, do you always feel this way when people ask you to read? Is reading always scary to you, especially when you have to do it in front of someone else?

C: I think so.

P: How come you can read calmly to your younger sister without becoming anxious?

C: (*She looks up and to the left.*) Because I enjoy reading to her!

P: Why?

C: Because she likes to hear those stories. She listens and even asks me to read a story to her. That makes me feel good.

P: What happens to your reading when you're feeling really good?

C: (*Looks up and to the left, and smiles.*) I read better!

P: What do you mean, you read better? Do you mean you read faster or smoother? Or, do you mean that you understand more of what you read?

C: Both!

P: Tell me more about this.

C: Well, when I'm reading to my sister, I don't worry about what she is going to think about how I read. I know that she likes me to read stories to her and it makes me feel pretty good. I guess this makes me read better.

P: What's the difference between you reading to your younger sister and reading aloud to your teacher?

C: Oh, when I read for my teacher I get very nervous and make a lot of mistakes, and the other children all laugh at me. (*This statement brings tears to her eyes and she begins to sob. Her dad moves over beside her and comforts her. He tells her that it's all right to feel sad because others make her feel bad.*)

P: Does anything else happen when you read to your teacher?

C: (*Still teary-eyed.*) Yes, she always corrects the words I don't say right. She tells me not to worry and to take my time. I feel like she thinks I take too long to read and I get really nervous.

P: Corinne, what would happen if you could feel good all the time when you read? Would that make it easier for you to understand what you read?

C: (*Looks up to the left, then straight down, smiles.*) Yes! If I could do that, I think I could understand what I read.

P: Well let me teach you a technique that you can use to help you gain control over these feelings. The technique will be your own special secret and will operate like a magic button. At any time you want to feel that way, you can press your magic button and have those good feelings. Or you might be able to squeeze your left fist and be able to get those feelings at any time.

[I explained to Mr. W. that Corinne's problems did not seem to be connected with any learning difficulty or disability but, rather, appeared to be associated with negative feelings that dramatically interfered with her reading abilities. The fact that she can read reasonably well to her younger sister, but not in the presence of adults, lends considerable support to this hypothesis. Somehow, reading out loud to adults has been negatively reinforced and she has begun to associate it with anxious feelings which override her cognitive processes. This certainly explains why she is able to engage in verbal discussions with her parents and to some extent in the classroom, although she appears shy and uncommunicative there.]

P: Before I teach that technique for learning how to feel good and maintain a sense of comfort while you are reading, I want you to do something else. I would like to have you read again, but this time I want you to read by holding the book up there (*demonstrates this by holding the book above eye level*). All right, go ahead.

[I listened to Corinne read and systematically compared it with the way she had read aloud a little earlier. On the initial reading, it was observed that Corinne placed the book on her lap, and looked down as she read. This particular reading posture seemed to be associated with slower speech, hesitancy, and less reading fluency. When she read in the awkward position of holding the book slightly above eye level, she displayed a smoother reading rate that incorporated emphasis and tonal shifts. I asked Corinne to stop and had her read again by holding the book on her lap. The results were identical to those perceived at the initial attempt. I again asked her to stop and to continue reading, holding the book above eye level. Not only did I see a marked difference between both postures, but so did her father. He commented on the obvious difference and asked for the reason for the change. I explained to him that the change in posture forced Corinne to shift her breathing patterns from the lower abdominal to her upper chest, and this shift created different physiological states.

Perhaps there was some merit to teachers, in earlier days, demanding that students ''sit up straight, shoulders back!'']

P: As you read that story, Corinne, did you detect changes in how you read?

C: Well, it felt better when I read up there. It seemed easier to do, but it was really hard to keep my arms up there.

P: Now, Corinne, what I'm going to ask you to do is to think of some really nice times in your life when you were feeling very good about yourself and about what you were doing. And as you begin to experience those feelings I want you slowly to close your left hand into a fist. You are only to close your hand in proportion to the intensity of your feelings. Let me explain that in a different way. Let's suppose your feelings are on a scale from one to ten, with one being a very weak feeling and ten being a very strong, positive feeling. A number five would mean that you are feeling fine, kind of in the middle. Now, if you are really, really feeling a strong, powerful feeling you close your fist all the way. Let me show what I mean by all of this. (*Demonstrates*) Good! Now I want you to close your eyes and think of a time when you did something you felt really good about. When you get that good feeling, you are to close your hand, depending on how strong that feeling is. Yes, that's right. (*Corinne begins to think, and after a while she closes her hand.*) Now let your hand open when the good feeling starts to leave. Good.

   Now Corinne, I want you to remember another time when you felt really good; when you felt calm, confident, or just plain happy. But this time, I want you to think of an experience that was stronger than the first one. Go ahead, close your eyes and get that special feeling. (*She accesses that positive feeling and gradually closes her hand and slowly lets it open again.*) That was really well done, Corinne. Now I want you to get another feeling, but this time it has to be stronger than the last one. Do you understand?

C: Yes.

P: As soon as you begin to get that feeling, start to close your hand, depending on how strong the feeling is. The stronger the feeling the more you close your hand. Now, go and get another remembered, positive experience. (*I watched how she responded to my directive by observing her muscle tones, breathing patterns, facial colorations and the eye movements underneath her eyelids, as well as her head tilts. This was done to ensure that she had pure access to the feeling state, to see if the patterns were similar to previous ones, and if they appear more intensified than before.*) Good, Corinne. What did all that feel like?

C: (*Corinne opens her eyes.*) It felt really good. I remembered a time when the family went to the beach. I really enjoyed swimming and playing in the water.

P: That's good. Let's test what you just did. I want you to close your eyes and begin squeezing your hand and tell me what happens on the inside. What are you aware of when you close your hand in just that special way? (*She shuts her eyes and closes her hand slowly.*)

C: I feel really good! I began to remember those good times, and that really made me feel good!

P: That's excellent, Corinne! So now, when you squeeze your hand or, rather, close it, you can get those good feelings whenever you want. It's like having your own special button that you can push to get those feelings at any time. Now let's test it a little further. I want you to think about reading out loud in the classroom, and as soon as you start to feel those old feelings begin to close your fist and get those new feelings. Now, go inside your head and remember a time when you stood up and read out loud in front of the class. As you think about this, and you begin to get those old feelings, close your fist tightly and tell me what happens.

C: (*She closes her eyes and, as she remembers those past feelings, her breathing shifts, her facial muscles tighten and her facial coloration becomes whiter. But as she begins to close her fist, there are noticeable changes in her facial coloration, breathing patterns and muscle tone. She takes a deep breath, looks surprised and then smiles.*) I see myself reading and not being afraid. There are some words I don't know, but I do the best I can. I feel really good.

P: Now you can open your fist, and then your eyes. That was really well done. I want you to remember to close your fist whenever you want to have those good feelings. All right?

C: Yes, I can do that!

P: Because I'm going to ask you to read out loud for me in a little while (*she begins to show signs associated with the old patterns*), and as you begin to feel those old feelings you can close your fist and feel those strong, positive and good feelings now. (*I waited to see how she responded to this suggestion, and noticed that her hand began to close, slowly at first, and then a little faster, until there was a definite smile.*) How did you feel about that request?

C: I feel fine. I really think that I can do it a lot better than before.

P: Well, here is the book, but before you begin to read you have to understand that you need to have your left hand free to be able to close it and to get those good feelings. So, I think you should perhaps hold the book in your right hand and as you begin to read out loud, whenever you want those (*points to her left hand*) feelings, you can just close your hand. Before you start, I want you to take a deep breath and then begin to read.

[I watched Corinne carefully as she started to read aloud. As soon as she showed signs of reverting to her past behavior, I reminded her to close her hand if she began to experience those old feelings. This repetitive process is done systematically to condition the old feelings as a stimulus for eliciting the new feelings.

Since, in her normal state, she naturally tenses herself by clinching her fist when reading, this natural gesture now becomes associated with good feelings. While the old feelings cue the new feelings, her old natural reflexive responses, clenched fists, naturally elicit the new feeling states and provide her with the necessary internal resources to read the story without any interference from her kinesthetic processes. As her dad and I looked on, it became apparent that there was a dramatic change in her reading ability. She was reading smoothly and much more fluently and at the same time continued to squeeze her fist tightly closed whenever she needed the new feelings. I watched her until she began to close her fist automatically every time she needed to.]

P: Just stop for a moment, Corinne. Tell me, what was different this time from the last time you read for me?

C: Well, I felt a lot better when I was reading, and whenever I started to get those old feelings I simply closed my hand and got the good feelings. It really felt good.

P: Good. I want you to read just a little more to see how you do. (*Corinne was asked to do this to see if she would engage the new associational cuing process on her own. She read much better and did not seem to rely on the cuing very much. She appeared to use it most often when she stumbled over a word or didn't know how to pronounce it.*) That was really excellent. Now there is one other thing I need to tell you. You can do this really well here and now, and I want you to practice it with your dad, at home. Is that all right? (*She nods affirmatively.*) The biggest step is to be able to use this new skill whenever you need it, especially in the classroom. So, I want you to close your eyes and imagine this new skill, just waiting to put it into practice. Can you see yourself doing this? (*She nods.*) As you are sitting comfortably at your desk, feeling safe and secure, the teacher calls your name and asks you to stand up and read a story. As soon as you hear this request you begin to experience that old feeling but then you remember what to do (*she begins to close her fist*) . . . and . . . (she begins to smile) smile, feeling those new positive feelings as you pick up your book and stand up, still feeling those new, powerful, pleasant and confident feelings. As you hold the book in your right hand, you take a deep breath and begin to read, feeling those new, good feelings and automatically closing your fist whenever you need those feelings. You may even take a moment to draw a deep breath, pause, close your fist if you need to, and continue to read. When you finish reading and sit down, I am sure you will continue to feel those good feelings and realize something of importance about yourself. Take a moment now Corinne, to rerun that experience in your mind, watching yourself stand up and read. When you are satisfied with what Corinne did in that movie version . . . you can change it to make it even better if you wish . . . open your eyes.

The next step was to instruct Corinne's father in the strategic procedure outlined above. He was also instructed to have Corinne follow this procedure every night while she read either to him or his wife. For the most part, he was advised to let Corinne determine its effectiveness. They were to come back in two weeks.

While this case history appears to represent a departure from the reading comprehension strategy outlined in this section, it was really preparatory. After the strategy was installed so that Corinne could automatically employ it in the most appropriate contexts, she was then taught the reading comprehension strategy. With her new-found resources, she had no problem learning to incorporate the reading comprehension strategy into the newly acquired techniques.

To implement the reading comprehension strategy without dealing effectively with Corinne's "kinesthetic interference" would, in my opinion, have been a disaster. The fact that her negative feelings were overriding her cognitive resources suggests how powerful they really were. Without interrupting her old patterns and installing new, more useful habits, Corinne would still be unable to read with any comprehension.

Corinne reported, at about the fourth session, that her teacher really complimented her on how well she was reading out loud in class. As she told this she could hardly contain herself. The parents also reported that the teacher had contacted them and wondered what they were doing to make such an improvement in Corinne's reading ability. As a result of the parents' comments to the teacher, I was asked to contact the teacher to explain the procedures to her. This I agreed to do, but only to tell the teacher about the reading comprehension strategy and how it could be reinforced within the classroom. The associational cuing or anchoring technique taught specifically to Corinne was not discussed with her teacher. It was decided by Corinne and I that this piece of information would be a secret between us. This request was respected in light of Corinne's effective use of the technique and her desire not to inform the teacher about this particular "magic button."

Follow-up for two years revealed that Corinne had overcome her reading comprehension difficulty and was performing academically at a satisfactory level, and slightly above her classmates. Her parents stated that Corinne was much happier than she had ever been and that she continued to read to her younger sister with renewed self-confidence. Furthermore, she began to read more books and could frequently be heard reading aloud at night. The parents reported also that, occasionally, she resorted to closing her fist and used the strategy whenever she felt she needed to!

TABLE 7
The Reading Comprehension Format

1. Read the Sentence or Paragraph (aloud or silently).

First, the teacher must make sure that the student can pronounce the words being read and understands their meaning. This is an important consideration because the student will be requested throughout this procedure to make associations with past experiences and previously acquired learning. Without this meaningful base to draw on, the student will be unable to generate a full external/internal representation of the story's content. Words should immediately stimulate some type of internal representation or automatically elicit an active and constructive accommodatory cognitive process to make sense out of what is being read.

2. Generate/Construct an Image.

After the student has read one sentence or paragraph, depending on his level of competence, he is to stop, look up right or left, and create an internal visual image of what was just read. (Students who have difficulty generating internal visual representations can draw them on paper.) As a teacher, you are not looking for artistic ability, but, rather, the student's ability to translate/transform the written word into some meaningful representation or schema. With this procedure, the student is free to employ stick figures to illustrate the content of what he has read.

The sole purpose of this particular step is to employ a cross-modal process of transforming incoming auditory information into a pictorial construction, representative, as accurately as possible, of the content.

3. Describe as Fully as Possible the Details of the Representative Picture.

This means that the teacher will need to instruct the student in how to gather the appropriate and most relevant bits of information effectively, and to incorporate the added data into the preliminary general picture. This is also an important step since, as he reads more sentences and paragraphs, the student will continue to revise and

TABLE 7 (Continued)

edit the contents of his initial image as he gleans more information about the story in terms of the characters, the setting, the sequence of events, and the plot.

At this point, the teacher can instruct the student in the process of gathering more complete information by using the self-questioning procedures. For instance, the student can be taught how to incorporate more fully representative data by answering the following basic questions:

a. Who? (Who are the characters involved in this story? Who is the hero or heroine?)

b. Where? (Where does the story take place?)

c. When? (When does the story take place?)

d. What? (What is the author attempting to do with this story? What is the story really about? What will likely happen at the end of the story?)

e. Why? (Why did the author write this story? For what purpose? Why is this a good/poor story?)

f. How? (How will the story end? How do you know this? How might the author have ended the story differently?)

Self-questioning is a method used to gather more information about the contents of a story (see Figure 18). However, before this step is taught, it is important that the student master the ability to transform the text into some meaningful, visual representation of the contents of the story.

Figure 18

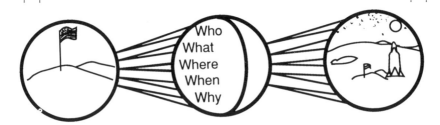

4. Evaluate the completeness and appropriateness of the picture.

Does it give the student enough information about the story so that he can make the necessary associations to develop some understanding of the story's content? What type of information does the student frequently miss or delete as he attempts to translate written text? More accurate data may be gathered by teaching the student to employ time frames (PAST, PRESENT, FUTURE) or temporal perspectives to develop

---

TABLE 7 (Continued)

a more complete translation. The student may search for the most useful information by attempting to establish connections between what has been read and his own personal history. The student can be taught how to gather more information to make sense out of what is being read, by employing five general sorting mechanisms:

a. Activities
The student thinks about the activities he has personally engaged in or vicariously participated in that are similar, structurally, to the events or activities related within the context of the story. He then attempts to use this personal experience to establish meaningful connections between himself and the events, actions and characters of the story. In other words, what is similar in the story to things he already knows or has some experience of to help establish a meaningful relationship with the story's content?

b. People
The student can think of people he knows in real life who resemble the characters in the story. He may find that a particular character manifests behaviors and mannerisms similar to someone in his life, such as a friend, a parent, a grandparent. This relationship will help the reader establish a particularly meaningful association with the story's content and, at the same time, facilitate the development of a more vivid and focused internal visual representation.

c. Places
The student can remember those places he may have visited that resemble the place talked about in the story. Using these personal memories of places he has visited or seen on television will make the places mentioned in the story become more real to him. He will also begin to realize that the places written about may, in fact, have a geographical basis in reality. This type of information certainly will help to establish a clearer image of the story's setting and the context within which the events take place.

d. Things
Along his journeys in life, the reader may have encountered objects that hold special significance for him. For some students, it may be a collection of old guns, stamps or rare artifacts. This type of information can be employed by the student to lend credence to the story's content. He may read about a piece of furniture that he recognizes and can tell others about. This would certainly increase his feelings of self-esteem.

e. Information
In his personal history, information about many things have been gathered through reading, listening to others, watching television or

TABLE 7 (Continued)

listening to the radio, that can be effectively used as a basis for making more sense out of what he is writing about. Some children like to watch science programs and thus know quite a bit about various species of flora and fauna and their habitats. This information may be most helpful in increasing the student's understanding of what is being read. In this procedure, the student is drawing heavily on his own resource bank and employing his own personal treasures to establish associations and connections to characters, places, events, things that will, in all likelihood, provide a meaningful basis for generating the ability to comprehend the written word.

In this way, he is establishing a personal link with the written material; a process which can only create further understanding and comprehension.

5. Repeat the Steps

Initially, the student should read only one sentence and go through all the above steps. When he has a good grasp of the procedures, he can graduate to more sentences and then to paragraphs. Some students find it easier at first, to use only phrases and attempt to generate images from them.

It is important to have the student move his eyes to the appropriate quadrants to generate the information that will be used to construct the internal image. The establishment of eye-movement patterns in conjunction with this procedure will help to reinforce the learning format as well as act as a natural cuing device for accessing the stored information. In a way, our eye-movement patterns are analogous to the access codes used to retrieve programs stored in computers. In fact, the use of eye-movement patterns allows the student to engage in a conscious process for retrieving and gaining access to previously acquired knowledge.

6. Automatizing the Strategy

Once the student has developed the strategy, so that he can read a story and simultaneously generate internal pictures that are as representative as possible of the story, he can develop more flexibility in how he manipulates the mental images. For instance, he can use the information gathered from the reading and generate a sequence of slides as if he were looking at a slide presentation. Or, he can develop his own movie version of the story. As an added learning device, the student can pretend that he is giving a running commentary about the story: what he sees, what he hears the characters saying, what they are feeling, and how they express themselves.

Once the strategy becomes automatic, the student should be able to read any story and simultaneously engage in other cognitive

---

TABLE 7 (Continued)

processes that add meaning to the story and thus facilitate the reader's understanding of the content. As the teacher, you should be able to evaluate the effectiveness and automaticity of the learning format by watching his eye-movement patterns or other external behavioral indices of cognitive functioning as he answers your questions about the story. Where does he move his eyes to access the necessary information to deal effectively with your questions? If the student seems to be having trouble in recalling the sequence of events or descriptions of the characters or settings, you may gently guide his eyes up to the appropriate quadrant to see if the information is stored there. This type of immediate and active feedback can also contribute to automatizing the reading comprehension format.

Mathematics
(Includes Arithmetic and Problem Solving)

P = Psychologist
M = Melanie

P: Melanie, your mother tells me that you are in Grade 3 and that you do very well in your school work. She also says that you are extremely good in mathematics. I asked your mom if I could speak to you today to find out what you do inside your head that makes you so good at mathematics. I hope that by figuring out what you do, I can then teach other students how to do the same thing. If I can teach them how you think when you do mathematics, then maybe they can learn to be more successful with their basic mathematics facts and how they solve mathematical problems. Do you understand all this?

M: Yes, kind of.

P: I'll be asking you some questions related to mathematical problems. I am not concerned about whether you give me right answers or not. What I am concerned about is how do you do it! What do you do inside your head that makes it possible for you to arrive at a solution? So there is no need for you to become worried or overly anxious, because I'm not concerned with your answer, only with how you did it. I will help you to understand what you do inside your head by asking you specific questions so that you BECOME AWARE of how you are THINKING. All right?

M: Yes, I think so.

P: Then let's do some things to give you an idea of what it is that I'm talking about. What is twelve plus six?

M: (*Melanie quickly looks up to the left*) Eighteen.

P: Correct. Now, Melanie, what did you do inside your head to get that answer? Did you see a picture of yourself doing this problem before or did you hear yourself solving it?

M: Oh, I just saw the answer.

P: You saw a picture of the answer inside your head? (*she nods*) Did you also see the equation twelve plus six in your head?

M: No.

P: So, you only saw the answer?

M: Yes.

P: All right then, what is nineteen plus eight?

M: (*Melanie looks up to her left but then quickly closes her eyes.*) Twenty-seven?

P: That's correct. What did you do inside your head to get the answer?

M: I saw it in my head, but it was not very clear.

P: What do you mean, it wasn't very clear? Were you able to make it clearer?

M: It was fuzzy at first, but then it got clearer. I think I closed my eyes to see it better.

P: That's excellent, Melanie, because that is exactly what I noticed. In fact, I was going to ask you why you closed your eyes, but you have just answered that. You closed your eyes to see the answer clearly. Did you talk to yourself about the question, or repeat it to yourself?

M: I don't think so.

P: What's four times six?

M: (*She looks up and left. The eye accessing cue is very rapid.*) Twenty-four.

P: How did you do that?

M: The same way as before. I just saw it in my mind and got the answer.

P: It sort of flashed in your mind and stayed long enough for you to see it clearly, and to give me the whole answer?

M: That's right.

P: All right. Let me ask you this question. If one chocolate bar costs eight cents, how much will three chocolate bars cost?

M: (*Melanie looks down to the left and exhibits noticeable subvocal movements. She looks up to the right and then up to the left. The latter eye movement is very similar to her previous eye movements.*) Twenty-four cents.

P: Excellent! Now how did you get that answer?

M: Well, I had to repeat the question to myself a couple of times. Let's see . . . (*looks up to the right*) I then saw myself writing the problem down on paper.

P: You mean that with your mind's eye you saw yourself writing the equation down on a paper? Were there feelings attached to this? That is, did you feel your hand moving as you wrote the equation down on paper?

M: No, I just saw myself writing it out. Then once I saw it written out on paper I knew that I needed to times eight by three to get my answer. Then I remembered that eight times three is (*looks up to the left*) twenty-four.

P: Solving this problem was much different from using simple basic facts. Whereas you just saw the answers immediately whenever I asked you some basic questions, when I asked you to solve this particular problem it required more effort. You used self-talk to repeat the question to yourself, then you saw yourself writing it out in equation form, realized what you had to do in order to solve it, and then quickly saw the answer. (*Melanie nodded as her mathematics strategies were verbally fed back to her.*) Let's try another problem. If one piece of candy costs four cents, how much will seven pieces of candy cost? And how much money will I get back if I give the cashier thirty cents? Just take your time.

M: (*Melanie looks down and to the left and subvocalizes, apparently repeating the question to herself. She then looks up and to the right as if staring off into space. Next, she looks momentarily up to the left.*) Twenty-eight cents.

P: That's right.

M: (*Melanie looks down left again, and then up to her left.*) Two cents.

P: That's great! Is it right to say that you did exactly the same as before with the first part of the problem? (*Melanie nods her head.*) I think that in order for you to solve the second part of the problem, you took some time to repeat the question to yourself, realized what you had to do, then looked up there (*points*) and saw the answer.

M: That's right.

P: Melanie, do you know what happens when you can't get an answer?

M: (*She looks up and to the left and then down, right.*) I think that the picture is fuzzy and that I can't see it.

P: So you see a very fuzzy picture? Do you ever not see any picture at all in your head?

M: (*Accesses up and to the left.*) Yes. My mind just isn't working, I guess.

P: So, your mind kind of goes blank? (*She nods.*) I want to thank
     you, Melanie, for allowing me to understand what you do inside
     your head when you remember your basic facts, as compared to
     what you do when you solve more complex problems. I learned
     that whenever you remember basic facts you look up and see the
     answer, but when you solve problems you repeat the question to
     yourself first and then see the equation appear in your mind, real-
     ize what it is that you have to do in order to solve it, and then
     see the answer inside your head. What I'm going to do now is
     to teach other children your strategies for learning basic mathe-
     matical facts and for solving more complex mathematical
     problems, to see if it makes it easier for them to learn how to do
     mathematics. And I really think it will!

This represents only a small part of the actual session. I had asked
Melanie many more questions than those cited in this example, so
that a well defined set of behavioral and cognitive patterns could be
detected and used to formulate a more efficient learning format for
remembering basic mathematical facts, and the development of a
general problem-solving strategy. Melanie was representative of many
children who are proficient in the mathematical skills. She displayed
the consistent behavioral responses and internal cognitive systems
that appear to be characteristic of students who possess good apti-
tudes for mathematics. How much of this is genetic and how much
is learned is debatable; however, my work and research with learning disabled students provides strong evidence that these cognitive
ability patterns can be elicited, explicated, notated and taught to other,
less able, students, with very good results. The methodology of *Cognitive Ability Patterning* requires the sensitity and sensory acuity
to detect behavioral responses that reflect internal cognitive systems
and information processing mechanisms. This requires training in the
area of cognitive psychology and observational skills. The learning
formats presented in this book will produce very positive results.

As you read the above transcript, you can appreciate the verbal and
behavioral descriptions offered by Melanie about her own internal
cognitive processes, and the psychological operations responsible for
her efficient performance in arithmetic and general mathematical
problem solving. Her behavioral descriptions are not an exception
but, rather, a common trait of arithmetical competence, shared by
many students with similar cognitive abilities. However, like Melanie,
some students, most noticeably learning disabled students, need to
be taught a language, or a set of verbal descriptions, that will allow
them to achieve a sufficient degree of metacognitive awareness to permit "cognitive cartographers" to explore more fully the dimen-
sions of "inner space", and, finally, to be able to delineate and

to specify the functional processes and the cognitive variables involved in generative learning. However, this step forward can only take place if individual students are active participants in the exploration process, and thereby teach us how to separate the map from the territory rather than pretend that we already know its shape, its contours and its geography!

Rationale for the Mathematics Format

Many learning disabled students have difficulties learning the "numbers tables" or the "basic facts" of arithmetic. A number of causes have been postulated to account for these mathematical deficiencies: inappropriate information processing systems (Torgesen & Kail, 1980; Resnick, 1976); verbal memory deficits (Tuoko, 1982); attentional deployment deficiencies (Ackerman, Anhalt & Dykman, 1986); emotional problems (Slade & Russell, 1971); procedural errors (Strang & Rourke, 1985).

The present mathematics learning formats include elements of several problem-solving mathematical models (Farnham-Diggory, 1968; Polya, 1945; Strang & Rourke, 1985; Walberg, 1980). These formats incorporate the research on imaginal cognitive processes (Levin, 1976; Paivio, 1971; Pressley, 1976) and verbal mediation strategies (Meichenbaum, 1977; Wittrock, 1981). Similarly, although not explicitly stated, the mathematics formats use the functional properties of the left and right hemispheres: sequential and simultaneous information processing styles (Kaufman, 1980).

While the basic arithmetic operations format employs the functional properties of the right hemisphere, simultaneity and gestalt patterning, the general mathematics problem-solving format attempts to integrate the capacities and abilities of both hemispheres. However, the latter format is somewhat skewed in the direction of left-brain processes; analysis, linearity and sequential processing.

Nathan: A Case History

Nathan is a Grade 4 student having difficulty remembering his basic mathematical facts, especially his multiplication tables. This not only led to computational and procedural errors but it was also creating severe frustrations resulting in tension headaches and abdominal disorders. In addition, his mother began to have difficulty in getting him to go to school in the morning. There was much crying along with many other psychological maneuvers designed to get his mother to give in and let him stay home. Intelligence tests revealed that he was above average in cognitive abilities (Full Scale IQ: 117). Interestingly enough, he performed within the average range on the arithmetic subtest of the *Wechsler Intelligence Scale for Children - Revised*. The administering psychologist found no apparent reason for his difficulty with mathematics. The results of the *Wide Range Achievement Test* revealed well-developed reading and spelling abilities, with an arithmetic score slightly below average. The psychologist attributed his less than optimal performance on the arithmetic subtest to mechanical errors: failure to read the sign appropriately or forgetting to carry.

The teacher's observations led to the hypothesis that Nathan did not know his basic facts. He was slow in responding to basic subtraction and addition, he was having quite a bit of difficulty with multiplication, and did not seem to understand the concept of division. She also felt that Nathan was a very bright boy who was verbally articulate, an exceptionally good reader, and very knowledgeable in certain areas. She had recommended resource room help and, while there was some improvement, he still lacked the basic facts.

A large part of the first interview with Nathan and his mother, Mrs. C., was spent in developing rapport with Nathan. Therapeutic metaphors (Gordon, 1978; Mills & Crowley, 1986) were employed to match Nathan's present anxieties and concerns, as well as to illustrate isomorphic examples of children or animals experiencing similar difficulties, and how they resolved them. After about forty-five minutes, the following conversation took place between Nathan and me.

P = Psychologist
N = Nathan

P: Nathan, I understand that you are having some difficulty with your mathematics facts. Your mom tells me you really want to learn them but find it very difficult. When I was in Grade 3, I had similar difficulties, until I learned a special trick. This trick taught me how to remember my basic facts so that I didn't need to think so hard about them. I have taught a lot of students who were having similar problems, and this same trick worked really well for them. However, there is one catch to it . . . you have to be really willing to practice it. If you agree to practice the trick, then I will teach you what it is. When you learn it, you will almost be like a transformer because you will be able to transform yourself into Math Man, who really can do mathematics! As a matter of fact, Math Man will be available to help the earthling called Nathan whenever he needs to know a particular mathematical fact. Are you game to learn this trick if I teach it to you?

N: All right.

P: Well then, before I teach you this trick I need to ask you some mathematical questions. I don't care about the answers, because what I really want to know is how you already do mathematics. Is that all right?

N: I guess so.

P: Nathan, I realize that this may scare you A LITTLE, but if you are willing to do this, then Math Man will be able to help you EVEN MORE.

N: All right.

P: I want you to do the best you can to answer the following questions, all right? (*Nathan nods.*) What is eight plus six?

N: (*Nathan immediately looks up to the right — he is right-handed — then down to his left, where he slowly counts out the answer on his fingers.*) Fourteen.

P: Good. Now, what is six plus eight?

N: (*Again Nathan looks up and to the right, then down to his left as he counts out the answer on his fingers.*) Fourteen.

P: Good, Nathan. Now when you solve my mathematics questions, what do you do inside your head to get the answers? Do you, for instance, see a picture of the numbers in your head, or do you talk to yourself and add up the numbers?

N: I use my fingers to figure out the answer.

P: I have a hunch that you also try to see a picture of the numbers in your head. By this, I mean that you look up there (*points*) and try to create a picture of the math equation six plus eight equals - and then figure out the answer by counting on your fingers.

N: Yes, but I don't get the answer up there!

P: That's all right. What is seven times four? (*Nathan again looks up to his right, then looks down to his left where he uses his fingers to count by fours.*)

[I had gathered enough information at this point to proceed to the next stage, that of installing a new learning format.]

P: Nathan, I want you to think about a transformer that you really like and can clearly see in your mind. That is, I want you to remember your favorite transformer and get a picture of him inside your mind. Go ahead and do that now.

N: (*Nathan looks up to the left, and immediately smiles.*) All right.

P: It looks as if you really can see him up there (*points*).

N: Yes, I can see inside my head. He's black, white and blue.

P: Good. Now let me teach you what he can do. Now Math Man can do something that you don't know he can do. I want you to look at this mathematics flash card ($9 + 8 = 17$) and I want you to pretend that your mind is like a camera and that Math Man can actually take a snapshot of this whole equation. When you can see the whole equation in your mind, then take it and put it inside Math Man's mouth! His mouth should be wide open so that you can see the whole equation. Tell me when you can do this.

N: (*Nathan looks at the flash card, then looks up and to the left. He again looks at the flash card and then up to the left. He does this several more times.*) Now I can see it clearly in Math Man's mouth.

P: Good. Now, I want you to look up there and have him close his mouth, (*Nathan does this.*) I want you to look up there again and ask "Math Man" to open his mouth to show that equation, and then tell it to me out loud.

N: (*Nathan looks up and to his left.*) Nine plus eight equals seventeen.

P: Good. Now look up there and see it again, only this time read it backward.

N: (*Nathan again looks up and to the left.*) Seventeen equals eight plus nine.

P: Excellent! It really must be a clear image or picture for you to be able to read it backward. That's great! So far so good, Math Man is beginning to learn how to do the trick that will make you into a math transformer. Let's do another one. Look at this flash card (7 X 4 = 28), and see it up there in Math Man's mouth. When you can see it clearly, have him close his mouth. Let me know when this is done. (*Nathan goes through a similar behavioral process to the one before, only this time it seems slightly faster.*)

N: O.K. I've got it!

P: Good. Now have Math Man open his mouth and give you the equation, then read it out loud.

N: Seven times four equals twenty-eight.

P: Excellent. Let's do some more.

[At this point, I spent about thirty minutes teaching Nathan some basic mathematical facts, mostly the multiplication table. When I thought Nathan had accumulated sufficient data, I decided to add a new part to the learning format.]

P: All right, Nathan, you have been doing very well. Now I'm going to teach you a little bit more before we end this session. You've learned a lot of the times table so I'm going to test you on it. (*Immediately Nathan's breathing pattern changes, his facial muscles become tense and he seems very anxious.*) I want you to stop for a moment, take a deep breath, and remember what Math Man can do! He has the answers, all you have to do is to look up there (*points*) whenever I ask a question, see Math Man open his mouth and give you the equation, and then you read off the answer. So take another deep breath and RELAX. Even more than that. Good. What is seven times four?

N: (*Nathan looks up to his left for a few seconds, then smiles.*) Twenty-eight.

P: That's correct! Now what is eight times four?

N: (*Nathan exhibits similar behavioral responses.*) Thirty-two.

P: Right. Now what is four times six?

N: (*Quickly looking up to his left.*) Twenty-four.

P: Six times three?

N: Eighteen.

P: Very good! How about four times five?

N: Twenty.

P: Let's see if I can trick Math Man. What is eight times three?

N: (*Nathan appears momentarily confused, but looks up to his left and seems to be searching for the answer. He finally pauses and smiles.*) Twenty-four.

P: You learned it the other way, but Math Man realized what I was doing. That's terrific! I think you should thank him for helping you to learn as much as you did today. Now we need to have you continue to develop Math Man's abilities. Remember, I said that you would have to be willing to practice the new magic trick.

N: Yes.

P: Are you still willing to practice it and to teach Math Man even more? In fact, I think he would like to learn as much as possible. But before I ask your mom to help you, are you willing to work with mom?

N: Yes.

P: Well, before I give your mom some instructions on teaching Math Man, I need to teach him one more trick; another kind of test. I am going to give you this piece of paper, but this time I'm going to say the equation, and you just write down the answer. However, before you write down the answer, what are you going to do?

N: I am going to look up and ask Math Man to open his mouth so that I can see the answer.

P: Good.

[At this point, I gave Nathan several mathematical questions and watched carefully to make sure the new mathematics strategy was occurring automatically; although at this point it was being consciously remembered.]

P: I'm really impressed with what Math Man has learned. If he keeps learning these facts as quickly as he has today, he'll know all of them in a month's time.

The remainder of the session was used to teach Mrs. C. how to help Nathan continue to learn the new mathematics format. She was told to work with Nathan for about twenty minutes every night, but to leave him sufficient time for play with his friends. It was also suggested that she give Nathan a test at the end of a week and that for every question Math Man got right, Nathan would receive a nickel. He could use the money earned by 'Math Man'' to treat himself and Math Man in some way. Nathan said that Math Man really liked this idea, but that he was afraid he would take all his mother's money!

I saw Nathan several more times and continued teaching him how to refine his new skill and adding some variety to Math Man's ability. Mrs. C. continued to work with Nathan and informed the teacher of this. After about three weeks, the teacher began to report considerable improvement in Nathan's performance. Whether or not he learned his facts within the month, as suggested hypnotically, was not known. After a two-year follow-up, his mother states that Nathan is doing very well academically. He doesn't talk any more about Math Man, but he is doing exceptionally well in his mathematics classes.

I have seen many learning disabled students who exhibit a disability called aculia or dyscalculia. From my clinical experience, this mathematics disability seems to be a function of over-reliance on the auditory system. As well, there is a strong tendency to use the fingers to solve mathematical problems. Since these students don't appear to employ visualization cognitive operations, they can usually be identified by giving them an equation to solve (such as $8 + 6 = ?$). They will use their fingers to arrive at the answer. When the same equation is fed to them in reverse these learning disabled students invariably resort to their fingers again to solve it. They do not see the relationship between the first and the second equation. That is to say, they do not employ the concept of reversibility and consequently do not recognize that the figures in the original question have simply been reversed and given to them again. It would seem that a possible prerequisite skill for the development and attainment of reversibility may be the capacity to see the relationship inside one's head.

Summary and Conclusions

This chapter has dealt at some length with the steps taken and the strategies used to help learning disabled students overcome learning deficits. More often than not, the postulated ability deficits turned out to be the deployment of inefficient and inappropriate information processing and cognitive systems. Thus, the formulation and the development of the learning formats were used to remediate specific strategy deficiencies manifested by many learning disabled students within certain subject areas: mathematics, spelling, reading comprehension, and creative writing. The results obtained by teaching the learning disabled students these new learning formats far exceeded my expectations.

While the learning formats were first systematically elicited from students who produced very positive results in specific subject areas, and then taught to learning disabled students, the formats themselves are grounded in cognitive psychology, cognitive behavioral methodologies and the neuroscientific research on the functional properties of the left and right brain. And even though these learning formats are predicated on research findings and theories, the most important thing about them, in my opinion, is that they work!

TABLE 8a
A Basic Arithmetic Format

Step 1.
Before teaching the learning disabled student the basic arithmetic format, you must systematically elicit the set of eye-movement patterns, or a specific eye-movement pattern that corresponds to the individual's long-term visual memory. This is best accomplished by asking the student a set of specific questions designed to access his "mind's eye." Usually, in normally organized right-handed children, the required eye movement will be up and to the left. However, this presupposition always needs to be checked out thoroughly.

Step 2.
Write on flash cards the basic facts to be learned. These should be written on the flash cards in the student's favorite color since this tends to reinforce the memorization of the basic facts as well as to act as a retrieval cue for accessing this information later on.

Step 3.
To begin the installation process, hold the flash card up the student's left. Have the student look at the arithmetical equation, and see it with his mind's eye. Then remove the flash card, and ask the student to look up and see the equation again with his mind's eye. Can he still see it clearly? For some students, this stage of the procedure requires special attention. You may need to teach a student that his mind is like a camera and, just like a camera, it can take a colored snapshot of the equation. When the student tells you that he can see it clearly, have him repeat it out loud so that you can gather the appropriate feedback in terms of evaluating the correctness of the arithmetical data. As a more sophisticated test, have the student read the equation backward. This will demonstrate the clarity of his internal image or picture. However, this last procedure should not be employed initially with students who manifest lateral or directional problems.

Step 4.
After the learning disabled student has learned several arithmetical facts, it is time to test the procedure by asking him the arithmetical equations and carefully monitoring his eye movements. As soon as you ask a question, the student should immediately look up and to the left, retrieve the internal image that he sees with his mind's eye, and give you the appropriate response. If the student does not do this

TABLE 8a (Continued)

automatically, then you must instruct him to look up to the left as he hears your question and before he responds to it. This is a very important and crucial step because many students attempt to fall back on their old cognitive strategies and corresponding eye-movement patterns to solve the arithmetical question. This cognitive habit must be stopped and the new format positively reinforced. Your aim is to install the new learning format so that it becomes as automatic as the old one. If the student seems to be having difficulty remembering the basic mathematical fact, then gently remind him to look up to the left to find it.

Step 5.
As the student becomes more proficient at visualizing mathematical equations and is responding efficiently and quickly to your questions, it's time to teach him to generalize this new ability and skill to writing. This is another crucial step, because you want the student to have quick access to the stored mathematical data as he is doing written arithmetical computations. In order to insure that these basic data are available during written work, you need to teach him how to use his eye movements to retrieve the information. So, give him a piece of paper and tell him that you are going to test him on the mathematical facts he has just learned; however, before he writes the answer down on the paper, he is first to look up and to his left, see the mathematical equation and the answer and then, and only then, write it down. Once he has written the answer down on the paper, he is to check his response by looking up left again and making sure that his answer is the correct one.

Step 6.
As a final step, you must teach the student how to generalize this new skill to the classroom. You can do this by leading him through a guided imagery exercise in which he sees and feels himself sitting at his desk. He then realizes that the teacher is giving him a mathematics quiz. He immediately writes down on his paper the numbers from one to twenty, and waits for the first question. For example, the teacher might ask what seven times eight equals. In response to this verbal stimulus, the student immediately remembers to look up to the left, see the equation clearly with his mind's eye, and then look at the correct answer before he writes it down beside one of the numbers. This procedure is done several times to future pace the newly acquired learning format efficiently.

The final piece of evidence you will need, to be really sure that the new learning format is appropriately and efficiently installed, is the automaticity of the eye movements. Whenever you ask the learning disabled student a specific mathematics question, there should be an

TABLE 8a (Continued)

automatic eye-movement shift to his upper left quadrant. This represents behavioral evidence that the new cognitive strategy is installed and that it is working automatically and unconsciously. This behavioral feedback lets you know how effective you have been in installing the new learning pattern. Any extraneous eye-movement pattern in response to a mathematical question signifies to you that the new strategy is not working, and in that event you will need to retrace the steps to refine the procedure further.

TABLE 8b
General Mathematics Problem-Solving Format

Step 1.
Read the problem ALOUD. The student is to read the problem aloud while the teacher makes sure that he understands the words being used to explain the problem. It must be borne in mind that the way to solve a particular mathematical problem for a learning disabled student is altogether different from having a student perform simple arithmetical computations. To engage a strategic problem-solving approach, the learning disabled student must be able to read the instructions and decode the meanings associated with the words. That is, the written words need to trigger off meaningful associations grounded on past experiences, present circumstances and future perspectives.

Step 2.
Have the student use external speech (in conjunction with appropriate eye-movement patterns) to PARAPHRASE THE PROBLEM: what it is; what needs to be done; what is presently known about the problem; and the most appropriate way to find a solution.

Step 3.
Visualize or Imagine: The student needs to search his memory to determine if previous learnings or existing knowledge bases can provide him with the means to solve the present problem, or, at the very least, provide a basis on which to develop a reasonable plan. Has he seen similar problems before? In what way? What information can the student use from his past learnings and experiences to help solve the problem he is facing now? If he has no memories to draw upon, then have him graphically sketch and/or schematically illustrate the problem. DRAW AN EXTERNAL REPRESENTATION OF THE PROBLEM STATEMENT.

TABLE 8b (Continued)

Step 4.
Develop a Plan of Attack: At this point, the student must hypothesize the best mode of attack. This he may do by brainstorming. Strategically, the plan of attack should be based on the information gathered in steps one to three, and, through the brainstorming process, he should be able to generate three potentially useful approaches to solving the problem.

Step 5.
Evaluate the Best Alternative Plan: Based on the brainstorming process, the student will be required to choose the plan most likely to succeed in solving the present mathematics problem.

Step 6.
Implement the Plan: The student will use the information obtained in the brainstorming process and the decision-making process to implement the most suitable solution to the problem. Next, the student actually carries out the mathematical computations involved in solving the problem.

Step 7.
Evaluate the Answer: After computing the answer, the student determines if the outcome is what he is after. (Does it look, feel and sound right?) This is an important step, because many learning disabled students do not seem able to evaluate the rightness or wrongness of an answer. If they have not developed internal criteria for knowing when something is right or wrong they will literally and consistently engage in trial and error maneuvers, never knowing when or if they have the right solution to the problem! If the answer to the first approach turns out to be wrong, then the student retraces his steps to the remaining two approaches to solving the problem, and implements one of them.

Suggested Exercises for Parents and Teachers

Many workshop participants requested further information on the kinds of questions to ask in order to observe crisp eye-movement patterns. From their own observations, they were aware that the "subject" would respond to some questions with several eye-movement patterns, while others would produce clearly discernable eye-movement. What made the difference? Why did some questions elicit multiple eye-movement patterns while others provoked singular or unilateral eye shifts?

To some extent, the brain has been conditioned to respond differentially to certain kinds of words. At the same time, there is a genetic predisposition for the left brain to respond more forcefully to verbal-linguistic inputs, while the right hemisphere reacts more quickly and efficiently to visual-spatial inputs. In other words, the two hemispheres of the brain have built-in attention sensors that respond in different ways to various types of environmental stimulation. Now, if the left brain responds more efficiently to sequential tasks, and the right to simultaneous tasks, then perhaps verbal descriptions of these innate neuropsychological processes will also activate the neuropsychological mechanisms in the appropriate hemisphere: i.e., sequential words may activate the cognitive processes of the left hemisphere, while simultaneously coded words will trigger the appropriate mental processes of the right hemisphere.

Similarly, the use of temporal predicates (past, present or future) will, generally, activate certain areas of the brain. Therefore, past predicates may automatically draw responses from the right hemisphere, while future or present tense words may activate responses from the left hemisphere. At the same time, a combination of the sensory modalities (visual, auditory, kinesthetic) with temporal predicates might produce a purer response from the executive hemisphere. If this assumption is correct, then it should be possible to detect eye shifts contralateral to the executive hemisphere being activated by the appropriate question. For example, the question "What color was your Grade 1 teacher's hair?" should elicit a left-eye movement, up and to the left.

The clearer your language in terms of temporal predicates, sequential and simultaneous words and sensory modality inputs, the greater the probability of observing crisp eye shifts. As well, unspecified words (think, know, aware, learn, understand, believe) will usually be coded in a particular system but not necessarily across individuals. Individuals predisposed to rely more on the right hemisphere may also code these unspecified words in the same hemisphere. So that when you ask a person to think about something, he will consistently respond with a set of eye-movement patterns appropriate to his way of processing information. There exists a large body of research that pooh-poohs the significance of eye-movement patterns. In fact, some researchers have claimed that there is no such thing! However, your experience in asking children and adults questions and then observing eye-movement patterns will definitely put this preposterous hypothesis to rest!

One other finding that clearly emerged from the workshops on eye-movement patterns was that questions, including more than two sensory cognitive systems or information processing strategies, frequently elicited several eye movements. This phenomena probably occurred as a result of the brain responding to the difference between input channels, representational or cognitive systems and output modes. So that, the question "As you listen to the sound of music, do you get a feeling for it?" not only elicits two separate eye movements, it also requires the recollection of a past experience associated with music, thereby activating a memory strategy also associated with a particular set of eye movements! Any time you observe a set of eye shifts that don't make sense to you, obtain some feedback about what that child or adult did inside his head. This type of information will provide you with valuable insights into the meaning of eye movements.

The questions that follow are designed to promote specific eye movement patterns. Before you ask the questions, read them over and predict what will happen in response to them. Will they prompt specific or pure eye shifts? Or will they access several eye movements? What will those eye movements be? As you compare your responses to the actual results, determine what made the difference. Only by engaging in these exercises with an attitude of curiosity will you learn to sharpen your observation skills and your ability to predict.

Visual Recalled
1. When you were five years old, what color was your favorite toy?
2. How do you spell the word school?
3. What does your room look like?
4. What was the color of your Grade 1 teacher's eyes?

Visual Constructed
1. In your mind, make a picture of a pink elephant with zebra stripes and green polka dots.
2. Imagine yourself with purple hair. What would you look like?
3. Make a mind picture of an orange popsicle covered with purple jam and green jelly?

Auditory Remembered
1. What does your favorite record sound like?
2. What sounds do you hear when you play an electronic game such as PAC-MAN?
3. What door in your house squeaks or closes the loudest? Softest?
4. Who in your family has the nicest/softest voice?

Auditory Constructed
1. What would the nursery rhyme "Mary had a little lamb" sound like backward?
2. Say the alphabet backward in your head.
3. In your own words what would you tell someone about _____?

Internal Dialogue
1. Go inside your head and ask yourself how old you are.

2. Repeat the nursery rhyme _____ inside your head.
3. What is the third word in the fourth line of "O Canada"?

Kinesthetic/Feelings
1. How do you feel right after your mom has yelled at you?
2. Do you remember how you felt inside the last time you were excited? Curious? Happy?
3. When you touch something rough like sandpaper, how does it feel?
4. How do you feel when someone asks you to spell?
5. How does it feel to have the warm sun on your exposed skin?

CHAPTER 6

THERE'S NO HEAVIER BURDEN
THAN A GREAT POTENTIAL

T HE INCREASING RESEARCH in learning disabilities substantiates one recurrent finding: there is no one theory that can explain adequately the nature of a learning disability. A learning disability is not a unitary phenomenon; each child is a unique individual with wide and varied developmental learning experiences. The learning disabled child's mind is a logical by-product of a set of learning experiences, genetic predispositions and neurological developments that innately bias and environmentally condition him to produce idiosyncratic styles of inputting, processing, organizing, representing and outputting information. In light of this, it is understandable that the accumulated research and theories on learning disabilities are inconclusive; unsubstantiated by conflicting and contradictory evidence on its etiology, diagnosis and remediation.

With this awareness of the individuality of each learning disabled child comes a professional and parental responsibility to understand the nature of this unique little person. To understand the learning disabled child fully, we will need to delineate the cognitive dynamics, the covert inner processes of thought, that generate the end products. We must not confuse the product with the process, but we must seek to understand the underlying thought mechanisms. We must learn to delineate the similarities and differences of thought patterns among students, and then learn to make of these cognitive and learning formats an effective learning pattern that will be available to all children.

In this final chapter, several organizing principles are proposed to help the teacher, the educator and the counselor to work more effectively with learning disabled students. These organizing principles will also assist the reader to synthesize the principles discussed throughout this book.

1. Meet the Learning Disabled Child in His Own Model of the World

To one extent or another, several researchers have implicitly addressed this principle (Bruner, 1966; Gaddes, 1980; Johnson &

Myklebust, 1967; Kaufman, 1979; Rourke, 1983, 1985; Sattler, 1982). Each learning disabled child accumulates a unique set of learning experiences that predispose him to perceive his world differently from that of others. These developmental experiences literally propel the learning disabled child to develop characteristic styles of knowing, learning, cognizing, mentating and behaving.

In accord with each child's personal history of development, growth and experience, wide and varied models of the world are constructed and internalized as definitive ways to interact with the environment. Because each learning disabled child's perceptions of the world is developmentally and experientially different, it follows that diagnostic and remedial procedures should be developed based on this principle. Knowing this, the person working with the learning disabled student needs to discover what that child can or cannot do. The person working with the learning disabled child must interact in such a way that a systematic profile of the child's strengths and weaknesses (cognitive systems, types of learning capability, information processing strategies, and so on) emerges. The child's characteristic styles of learning, thinking and cognizing are used by the teacher to remediate the actual problem.

Korzybski's (1973) principle that the "map is not the territory" can be used to expand upon the above ideas. Each individual, in accordance with his personal history, develops a model of the world that guides his behaviors and responses. Like the human fingerprint. No two models of the world are exactly alike. There may be some similarities, but there will also be profound differences in terms of perception and representation. For a learning disabled child, the problem arises when he believes the map *is* the territory. This position precludes the learning disabled student from operating out of sensory experience; that is, paying attention to certain modality aspects of the environment and using the feedback to make changes in his internal model. For many learning disabled children, this rigid attachment to a specific model of the world prevents them from using the flexible, adaptable capacities of their brain. In essence, they become Skinner's black box; mere creatures of habit and conditioning. This represents a *no choice* scenario, or a "more of the same" approach (Watzlawick, Weakland & Fisch, 1974).

Our task as professional educators is to meet the learning disabled child in his own model of the world as it pertains to the context of learning and academic achievement within the educational arena. This requires the teacher to take the time to learn what goes on in the learning disabled child's head; how he learns to do things (which may be different in each subject area); what strategies he uses to code, organize and represent incoming information; and how to use the learning disabled child's assets to effect change. Until we stop imposing our theories and our models of the world onto the learning disabled child, along with our particular ways of interacting with the environment, learning disabilities will continue to increase at an exponential rate.

2. Theories Are Not the Learning Disabled Student

Theories abound attempting to explain the aetiological factors responsible for learning disabilities. These theories run the whole gamut, from neurological and neuropsychological deficits to information processing dysfunctions to maturational lag disorders. Yet, Ross (1980) states: "The field of learning disabilities is long on theory and short on fact." This does not mean that theories are, in and of themselves, worthless. Theories are developed to assist us in our understanding of the learning disabled child's model of the world. By the same token, this means that theories are only partial truths and, by implication therefore, partial lies. When we reify the theory or the theorists we literally put on perceptual blinkers that narrow our options and constrict our efficiency in working with learning disabled students.

Theories that touch upon learning are well-intentioned attempts to advance our knowledge about various aspects of human behavior. They try to explain the underlying reasons for learning problems as well as provide us with diagnostic and remedial interventions. Yet, many professionals seem to forget that theories are, for the most part, hypothetical constructs developed to explain the possible reasons for some learning disorders. They tend to forget that they are working with a living, unique human being - the *only* human being who can provide them with vitally important information about the nature of his or her learning disability. Perhaps, as Milton Erickson (Lankton, 1983) so eloquently put it, we should invent a new theory and a new approach for each individual learning disabled child.

3. The Learning Disabled Student Is Doing the Best He Can Under Present Conditions.

Most theories predispose teachers and educators to view the learning disabled child in terms of what he cannot do. This negative emphasis on learning deficiencies precludes the teacher from meeting the child on his own ground, his model of the world. It literally prevents the teacher from understanding that the learning disabled child is doing the best he can, given the nature of his or her personal history and past learnings.

The concept of the "broken child" pervades many educators' thinking about the lack of abilities and capacities within the learning disabled student. In a real sense, this deficit model compares the learning disabled child to a broken car. The car is taken to a specialist, called a mechanic, who, with sophisticated and advanced electronic equipment and mechanical gadgetry, is able to diagnose the problem. Once the problem is pinpointed, the malfunctioning part is replaced and the car once again runs smoothly and efficiently. But a child is not a broken car. A learning disabled child does not enter this world with replaceable parts. What he has is all that child is going to get!

Our first task as educators is to recognize that the learning disabled child is doing the best he can *at this time.* Our second task is to analyze what he has going for him in terms of strengths and assets. Then third, we need to use the child's strengths to expand his model of the world; that is, his internal map of learning systems and cognitive strategies.

4. Respect All Learning Systems and Modalities

Gardner (1983) has adequately addressed this important issue. There are many forms of intelligence, as well as numerous types of learning and cognitive styles. And each form or style is the direct by-product of a child's personal history and past learning experiences. For some learning disabled children, their learning systems do not fit in well with the cognitive and intellectual demands of the school environment. Does this mean that the educational system has a patent or a monopoly on what constitutes *the right way* to learn?

Bruner (1966), Piaget (1963), Montessori (1967), Luria (1973) and Kaufman (1979), to one extent or another, realized the importance of understanding and accepting a child's preferred learning system and how he organizes, codes and represents incoming information. How the child translates and then transforms incoming information seems to be a necessary and prerequisite step for effective and efficient learning to develop. Vera John Steiner (1985:8) illustrates this in the following way:

> The choice of such a language, or inner symbol system, is not always a conscious one. It is embodied in the history of an individual, beginning with his or her efforts at reflection that first developed in childhood. But the transformation of what is heard, seen, or touched is dependent upon the individual skill of the human mind in representing experience as images, as inner speech, as movement ideas. Through these varied languages of thought, the meanings of these experiences are stored and organized.

Thus, the ability of the child to code, organize and transform incoming instruction into the "varied languages of thought" - images, inner speech and movement (kinesthetic) ideas - will determine the extent to which he learns within any context. To a large degree, the variety of ways that a child has "available for processing or organizing incoming information" (Almy, 1964) can set limits on intellectual growth. This ability to transform input stimulation into images, inner speech or movement ideas seems to be the basis, the structural and process component, responsible for the intellectual and cognitive growth of an individual child. This position is adequately addressed by Dilts (1980:17) in his discussion of Bandler and Grinder's (1979) cognitive-behavioral model:

> The basic elements from which the patterns of human behavior are formed are the perceptual systems through which the members of the species operate on their environment: vision (sight), audition (hearing), kinesthesis (body sensations) and olfaction/gustation (smell/taste). The neurolinguistic programming model presupposes that all of the distinctions we as human beings are able to make concerning our environment (internal and external) and our behavior can be carefully represented in terms of these systems. These perceptual classes constitute the structural parameters of human knowledge . . .

> In Neurolinguistic Programming, sensory systems have much more functional significance than is attributed to them by classical models in which the senses are regarded as passive input mechanisms. The sensory information or distinctions received through each of these systems initiate/modulate, via neural interconnections, an individual's processes and output. Each perceptual class forms a sensory-motor complex that becomes response-able for certain classes of behavior . . .

The study of epistemology, how you know that you know, suggests that in order for us to be effective in developing remedial interventions and individual educational plans that work, we must understand how the learning disabled child learns, thinks and develops. In other words, we must be able to delineate and to specify the learning disabled child's learning systems, cognitive styles and mental modes of processing information before we can justifiably develop remedial procedures. Without this information we are metaphorically wandering through a labyrinth, with no geographical map and no idea where our wanderings will lead us. We could theoretically spend the rest of our lives wandering through this complex maze.

Once we understand the significance of the "varied languages of thought", then as part of the curriculum program we need to learn how to arrange the classroom environment so that these cognitive systems and mental processes are naturally nurtured, fostered and developed. As educators and teachers, how can we arrange the educational environment in such a way, in terms of activities, tasks and play, as to elicit and develop the child's innate potentialities? Can these skills and abilities be developed indirectly without the child knowing that learning is taking place? This means that we would have to analyze the tasks and activities in terms of what cognitive systems and information processing modes are necessary to complete the assignments. By the same token, we would need to understand exactly what systems are being developed by particular educational tasks and activities. Our whole curricular approach to education would need to shift priorities, from content to process. Or would it?

In the movie *The Karate Kid*, Daniel wanted to learn karate. He asked a Japanese neighbor, Mr. Miyagi, to teach him how. Miyagi agreed to teach Daniel if he would commit himself to following Miyagi's teachings. What we see happening, or so our first impressions tell us, is Daniel doing all types of routine jobs for Miyagi. He washes the car and paints the fence, as well as other prescribed tasks. We begin to believe that Daniel is being taken advantage of. And so does Daniel! However, during a confrontation with Miyagi, Daniel discovers that he was indeed learning, without being aware that he was being taught. Miyagi shows him what he has learned through doing the seemingly boring tasks. He has learned specific karate moves: blocks. Daniel leaves the confrontation with the conscious awareness of his new-found skills; with a sense of accomplishment, and a commitment to continue his learning.

5. A Learning Disabled Child Cannot Not Learn

All children learn, but some learn differently from others. Gardner (1983) and others have delineated the various types of intelligence that one child can exhibit, and the concomitant learning and cognitive styles that arise and grow out of these proclivities. Learning disabled children *can learn in their own way*. Our task as educators, teachers and parents is to identify what this way is, and then to use it to teach them to be more effective learners.

It is vitally important for us to realize that the learning disabled child can learn regardless of neurological impairments, maturational delays, neuropsychological deficiencies or unknown learning disabilities. The capacities of the brain to adapt are only now becoming understood through the research in the neurosciences. This field holds a promising future for the learning disabled child. But until other insights and new techniques are evolved, our task is to help the learning disabled child—NOW—to become a fully functional individual.

This requires professionals who will meet the child at his model of the world; who will invent and develop new approaches to working with learning disabled youngsters. It requires educators who will understand that learning disabled children cannot *not* learn; that they have abilities and capacities not yet tapped. In order to bring about permanent change so that these children can learn in school, at home or in society, we must be willing to go beyond what the theories propound. We must be willing to use those techniques, strategies and tasks that work.

And we must learn, from the children themselves, *how* they learn. We must constantly ask ourselves how it is possible for a child not to learn. What goes on in a child's head that he cannot spell, read, write or do mathematics? As educators and teachers, we need to remind ourselves continually of the philosophy of Charlie Brown who so succinctly said: ''There is no heavier burden than a great potential!''

REFERENCES

CHAPTER 1

Bateman, B.D. (1965) An Educator's view of a diagnostic approach to learning disorders. *In Learning Disorders, Volume 1*, Editor: J. Hellmuth. Seattle: Special Child Publications.

Bogen, J.E. (1975:17, 24-32) Some Educational Aspects Of Hemispheric Specialization. *UCLA Educator*.

Brown, L.F. Kraly, J., & McKinnon, A. (August/September, 1979:480-482) Resource Rooms-Some Aspects to Ponder. *Journal of Learning Disabilities*.

Bruner, J. & Oliver, R.R. (1967) *Studies in Cognitive Growth*. New York: John Wiley & Sons.

Chall, J.S. & Mirsky, A.F. (1978) *Education And The Brain:* The Seventy-seventh Yearbook of the National Society for the Study of Education. Chicago: The University of Chicago Press.

Davis, M. W. (1982) *The Role of Vision in the Multidiciplinary Approach to Children with Learning Disabilities.* Springfield, Ill. Charles C. Thomas Publishing Company.

Dunn, L.M. (1968:35, 5-22) Special education for the mildly retarded: Is much of it justifiable? *Exceptional Children.*

Farnham-Diggory, S. (1978) *Learning Disabilities* Massachusetts: Harvard University Press. Federal Register,(Thursday, 29 December, 1977, 65082-65085), Washington D. C.

Feuerstein, Reuven. (1979) *The Dynamic Assessment of Retarded Performers: The Learning Potential Assessment Device, Theory, Instruments, and Techniques.* Baltimore: University Park Press.

Feuerstein, Reuven (1980) *Instrumental Enrichment: An Instrumental Program for Cognitive Modifiability.* Baltimore: University Park Press.

Flax, N. (1972) *The Eye and Learning Disabilities*, Journal of the American Optometric Association. Vol. 43, no. 6, 1972.

Gazzinga, M. S. (1975: 17, 9-12) Recent Research on hemispheric lateralization of the human brain: Review of the split brain. UCLA *Educator*.

Getman, G.N. (November 1985: Volume 18, number 9, pp 505-512) *A Commentary on Vision Training*.

Gordon, W. J. & Poze, T. (1979) Learning Dysfunction and Connection Making. *In the Metaphorical Way of Learning and Knowing*. Cambridge: SES Associates.

Geschwind, N. (1985: volume 457) Mechanisms of Change after Brain Lesions. In *Hope For a New Neurology: Annals of the New York Academy of Sciences*.

Hammill, D. D. (1972 6, 349 - 354) The resource room model in special education. *Journal of Special Education*.

Hammill, D. D., Leigh, J., McNutt, G. & Larsen, S.(1981: 4) A new definition of learning disabilities. *The Learning Disability Quarterly*.

Hunt, D. E. & Sullivan, E. V. (1974) *Between Psychology and Education Hinsdale*: The Dryden Press.

Huxley, A. L. (1942) *The Art of Seeing* New York: Harper's Bros., Johnson, D.J. & Myklebust, H.R. (1967) *Learning Disabilities: Educational Principles and Practices*. New York: Grune & Stratton.

Keogh, B.K. & Pelland, M. (April 1985, Volume 18, number 4, pp 229-236) *Vision Training Revisited*. Journal of Learning Disabilities.

Kinsbourne, M. & Caplan, P. (1979) *Children's Learning and Attention Problems*. Boston: Little, Brown.

Kirk, S.A. (1962) *Educating Exceptional Children*. Boston: Houghton-Mifflin.

Kirk, S.A. & Bateman, B. (1962: 29, 73-78) Diagnosis and remediation of learning disabilities. Exceptional Children.

Kriskin, R. A. (1973) *How to Improve Your Vision* N. Hollywood, CA. Wilshire Book Company.

Lerner, J. (1981) *Learning Disabilities: Theories, Diagnosis, and Teaching Strategies*. Botson: Houghton-Mifflin.

MacDonald, L. W. (1962-1965) *Visual Training Procedures. The Optometric Extension Program*. Santa Ana, CA.

Myers, P.I. & Hammill, D.D. (1982) *Learning Disabilities: Basic Concepts, Assessment Practices, and Instructional Strategies*. Austin, Texas: ProEd.

Myklebust, H.R. (1963) Psychoneurological learning disorders in chilren. In S.A. Kirk & W. Becker (Eds), *Conference on Children with Minimal Brain Impairment*. Urbana: University of Illinois Press.

Myklebust, H.R. (1968) Learning disabilities: Definition and overview. In Progress in Learning Disabilities Vol.1. Edited by H.R. Myklebust. New York: Grune & Stratton.

Ornstein, R. (1972) *The Psychology of Consciousness*. New York: The Viking Press. Ornstein, R. (May, 1978) The Split and the Whole Brain. *Human Nature*.

Parrill-Burnstein, M. (1981) *Problem Solving and Learning Disabilities: An Information Processing Approach*. New York: Grune & Stratton.

Pierce, J. R. (September 1983, Volume xiv, number 3, whole issue). Annual Review of The Literature. Journal of Optometric Vision Development.

Roby, A. (1983) *Developing Visual Skills, a program of Vision Activities for use in the school setting.* Developmental Vision Project, ESEA Title IV-C, Fountain Valley, CA.

Ross, A.O. (1976) *Psychological Aspects of Learning Disabilities & Reading Disorders.* New York: Grune & Stratton.

Ross, A.O. (1980) *Learning Disability: The Unrealized Potential.* New York: McGraw-Hill Book Company.

Rourke, B.P., Bakker, D.J., Fisk, J.L. & Strang, J.D. (1983) *Child Neuropsychology: An Introduction to Theory, Research, and Clinical Practice.* New York: The Guildford Press.

Sattler, J.M. (1982) *Assessment Of Children's Intelligence And Special Abilities.* Boston: Allyn and Bacon, Inc.

Schrock, R. E. (1968 - 1972) *Dragnosis, Prognosis and Techniques in Visual Training.* Optometric Extention Program. Santa Ana, CA.

Smith, C.R. (1983) *Learning Disabilities: The Interaction of Learner, Task and Setting.* Boston: Little, Brown and Company.

Wittrock, M.C. (1977) *The Human Brain.* New Jersey: Prentice-Hall

Wittrock, M.C. (1981) Reading Comprehension. In *Neuropsychological and Cognitive Processes in Reading.* Editors: Pirozzolo, F. J. & Wittrock, M. C.. New York: Academic Press.

CHAPTER 2

Almy, M. (1966) *Young Children's Thinking: Studies of some aspects of Piaget's theory.* New York: Teachers College Press.

Atwood, B.S. (1975:8, 72-78) Helping students recognize their own learning styles. *Learning.*

Andreas, C. (1983) The Relationship of Eye Movements while Information Processing Sensory Mode. Unpublished doctoral dissertation, Universtiy of Colorado.

Bakan, P. (1969: 28, 927-932) Hypnotizability, laterality of eye movements, and functional brain asymmetry. *Perceptual and Motor Skills.*

Bakan, P. (1971: 4, 64-69) The eyes have it. *Psychology Today.*

Bandler, R. & Grinder, J. (1975) *The Structure of Magic, Volume 1: A Book About Language and Therapy.* Palo Alto, CA: Science and Behavior Books.

Bandler, R. & Grinder, J. (1975) *The Structure of Magic, Volume 11.* Palo Alto, CA: Science and Behavior Books.

Bandler, R. & Grinder, J. (1975 and 1977) *Patterns of the Hypnotic Techniques of Milton H. Erickson, M.D. Volumes 1 and 11.* Cupertino, CA: Meta Publications.

Barbe, W. & Swassing, R. (1978) *Teaching through Modality Strengths: Concepts and Practices.* Columbus, Ohio: Zaner-Blosser, Inc.

Beck, C. and Beck, E. (1984: 58, 175-176) Test of Eye Movement Hypothesis of NLP: a Rebuttal and Conclusions. *Perceptual and Motor Skills.*

Bogen, J.E. (1975: 17, 24-32) Some Educational Aspects of Hemispheric Specializations. *UCLA Educator.*

Bruner, J. (1960) *The Process of Education.* Cambridge, Mass.: Harvard University Press.

Bruner, J. (1964: 19, 1-15) The course of cognitive growth. *American Psychologist.*

Bruner, J. (1966) *Studies in Cognitive Growth*. New York: John Wiley & Sons, Inc.

Camp, B.W. (1977: 86, 145-153) Verbal Mediation in young aggressive boys. Journal of Abnormal Psychology.

Cassirer, Ernest. (1970) *An Essay On Man*. New York: Bantam Books.

Cassirer, Ernest. (1974) *The Problem of Knowledge*. Clinton, Mass.: The Colonial Press Inc.

Chall, J. & Mirsky, A. (Eds) (1978) *Education And The Human Brain*. National Society for the Study of Educational Yearbook.

Cole-Hitchcock, S.T. (1980: 41(5): 1908B.) A Determination of the Extent to Which a Predominant Representational System Can Be Identified Through Written and Verbal Communication. Doctoral Dissertation, Baylor University, 1980. *Dissertation Abstracts International*.

Conway, F. & Siegelman, J. (1983: 91(9)) The Awsome Power of the MIND-PROBERS. *Science Digest*.

Das, J.P., Kirby, J. & Jarman, R. F. (1975: 82,99) Simultaneous and Successive Syntheses: An Alternative Model for Cognitive Abilities. *Psychological Bulletin*.

Das, J.P., Kirby, J. & Jarman, R.F. (1979) *Simultaneous and Successive Cognitive Processes*. New York: Academic Press Inc.

Day, M. (1964: 19, 443-446) An eye movement phenomenon relating to attention, thoughts, and anxiety. *Perceptual Motor Skills*.

de Bono, E. (1967) *The Use of Lateral Thinking*. New York: Penguin Books.

de Bono, E. (1969) *The Mechanism of Mind*. New York: Penguin Books.

Dilts, R. (1977) EEG and Representational Systems. Palo Alto, CA: Meta Publications.

Dilts, R. (1980) *Neurolinguistic Programming, Volume 1: The Study of Subjective Experience*. California: Meta Publications.

Dorn, F.F. (January, 1983: 22, 30) The Effects of Counselor Client Predicate Use Similarity on Counselors Attractiveness. *Americal Mental Health Counselors Association Jr.*

Duke, J. (1968: 78, 189-195) Lateral eye movement behavior. *Journal of General Psychology*.

Dunn, R. & Dunn, K. (1977: 87, 122-144) How to diagnose learning styles. *Instructor*.

Dunn, R. & Dunn, K. (1979: 36, 238-244)

Learning Styles/Teaching Styles: Should they...can they...be matched? *Educational Leadership*.

Elkind, D. & Flavell, J.H. (Eds). (1969) *Studies In Cognitive Development: Essays in Honor of Jean Piaget*. New York:Oxford University Press.

Ellickson, J.L. (1981:41(7): 2754B) The Effects of Interviewer Responding Differentially to Subjects' Representational Systems as Indicated by Eye Movement. Doctoral dissertation, Michigan State University, 1980. *Dissertation Abstracts International*.

Ellickson, J.L. (1983:30, 339-345) Representational Systems and Eye Movements in an Interview. *Journal of Counselling Psychology*.

Erhlichman, H., Weiner, S., & Baker, A. (1974: 12, 265- 277) Effects of Verbal and Spatial Questions on Initial Gaze Shifts. Neuropsychologia.

Flaro, L. (1986: Vol 15, no 2.) An Evaluation of the NLP Spelling Strategy with Learning Disabled Students. *Teaching Atypical Students in Alberta.*

Flaro, L. (1987:December) The Development and Evaluation of a Reading Comprehension Strategy with Learning Disabled Students. Reading Improvement.

Flaro, L. Eye Movement Patterns as a possible predictor of Verbal-Performance Discrepancies on the WISC - R (in preparation).

Flavell, J. (1963) *The Developmental Psychology of Jean Piaget.* New York: D. Van Nostrand Company.

Gazzaniga, M.S. (1975: 17, 9-12) Recent research on hemispheric lateralization of the human brain: Review of the Split-brain. *UCLA Educator.*

Harber, R. (1969, April: 220, 4) Eidetic images. *Scientific American*

Harnett, D. (1974: September 27) The Relation of cognitive style and hemispheric preference to deductive and inductive second language learning. Paper presented at the Neuroscience meeting, Brain Research Institute, UCLA.

Hernandez, V.O. (1981: 42(4): 1587B) A study of Eye Movement Patterns in the Neurolinguistic Programming Model. Doctoral dissertation, Ball State University, 1981. *Dissertation Abstracts International.*

Hunt, D.E. (1971) *Matching Models in Education* Toronto: Ontario Institute of Studies in Education.

Hunt, D.E. & Sullivan, E. (1974) *Between Psychology and Education.* Illinois: The Dryden Press.

Hunt, J.McV. (1961) *Intelligence and Experience.* New York: The Ronald Press Company.

Inhelder, B.. Sinclair, H. & Bovet, M. (1974) *Learning and the Development of Cognition.* Cambridge, Massachusetts.

Kaufman, A. & Kaufman, N. (1983) *Kaufman Assessment Battery for Children: Interpretive Manual.* Circle Pines, Minnesota: American Guidance Service, Inc.

Kaufman, A. (1980) Kaufman Assessment Battery for Children (K-ABC). Psycan, Inc.

Kinsbourne, M. (1972: 176, 539-541) Eye and Head Turning Indicates Cerebral Lateralization. *Science.*

Kinisbourne, M. (1974: 12, 279 - 281) Direction of Eye Gaze and Distribution of Cerebral Thought Processes. *Neuropsychologia.*

Kocel, K., Galin, D., Ornstein, R., & Merrin, E. (1972:27, 223-224) Lateral Eye Movement and Cognitive Mode. *Psychonomic Science.*

Lawrence, Gordon. (1984) *People Types and Tiger Stripes.* Florida: Centre for Application of Psychological Types, Inc.

Lerner, J.W. (1976) *Children with learning disabilities* (2nd Ed). Boston: Houghton-Mifflin.

Levine, M., Brooks, R., & Shonoff, J. (1980) *A Pediatric Approach to Learning Disorders.* New York: John Wiley & Sons.

Luria, A.R. (1978) *The Working Brain.* Toronto: Penguin Books.

Luria, A.R. (1980) *Higher Cortical Functions In Man.* New York: Basic Books, Inc., Publishers.

Luria, A.R. (1982) Cognitive Development: Its Cultural and Social Foundations. Cambridge, Massachusetts: Harvard University Press.

Mace, S. (1982, March 22: 8) The Eyes Have It: NLP Learning Theories Inspire Spelling Program. *Infoworld.*

McCarthy, B. (1980) *The 4MAT System: Teaching to Learning Styles with Right/Left Mode Techniques.* Illinois: Excel, Inc.

Meichenbaum, D. & Goodman, S. (1971: 77, 115-126) Training Impulsive Children to Talk to Themselves: A means of Developing Self Control. *Journal of Abnormal Psychology.*

Meichenbaum, D. (1977) *Cognitive-Behavior Modification: An Intregrative Approach.* New York: Plenum Press.

Miller, G., Galanter, E. & Pribram, K. (1960) *Plans and the Structures of Behavior.* New York: Holt, Rhinehart & Winston, Inc.

Ornstein, R.E. (1972) *The Psychology of Consciousness.* New York, The Viking Press.

Ornstein, R.E. (1978, May) The split and the whole brain. *Human Nature.*

Owens, Lee. (1977) An investigation of eye movement and representational systems. Unpublished doctoral dissertation, Ball State University, Muncie, Indiana.

Peale, R. (1980) The Testing of a Model for the Representation of Consciousness. The Fielding Institute.

Rosner, J. (1979) *Helping Children Overcome Learning Difficulties* (2nd Ed). New York: Walker And Company.

Segalowitz, Sid., (1983) *Two Sides of the Brain: Brain Lateralization Explored.* Englewood Cliffs, N.J.: Prentice-Hall, Inc.

Shaw, D. (1977) Recall as Effected by the Interaction of Presentation: Representational Systems and Primary Representational System. Unpublished doctoral dissertation, Ball State University.

Skinner, B.F. (1979) *Science and Human Behavior.* New York: The Free Press.

Sokolov, A.N. (1975) *Inner Speech and Thought.* New York: Plenmum Publishing Corporation.

Thomason, T.C., Arbuckle, T. & Cody, D., (1980: 51, 230) Test of Eye-Movement Hypothesis of Neurolinguistic Programming. *Perceptual Motor Skills.*

Vygotsky, L. (1975) *Thought and Language.* The Massachusetts Institute of Technology.

Williams, L.V. (1983) *Teaching for the Two Sided Brain.* Englewood Cliffs, N.J.: Prentice-Hall, Inc.

Wittrock, M.C. (Ed.) (1980) *The Brain and Psychology.* New York: Academic Press, Inc.

CHAPTER 3

Bateman, B. (1968) The efficacy of an auditory and a visual method of first grade reading instruction with auditory and visual learners. In *Perception and Reading,* edited by H.K. Smith, Newark, Delaware: International Reading Association.

Boder, E. (1982) *The Boder Test Of Reading-Spelling Patterns: A Diagnostic Screening Test for Subtypes of Reading Disability.* New York: Grune & Stratton.

Camp, B. & Bash, M. (1982) *The Think Aloud Program.* University of Colorado Medical School.

Flaro, L. (1986: 15, 2, 18-23) An Evaluation of the NLP Spelling Strategy with Learning Disabled Students. *Teaching Atypical Students in Alberta.*

Garfield, C. (1984) *Peak Performance: Mental Training Techniques of the World's Greatest Athletes.* New York: Warner Books, Inc.

Ingram, T., Mason, A. & Blackburn, I. (1970: 12, 271-279) A retrospective study of 82 children with reading disability. *Developmental Medicine and Child Neurology.*

Johnson, D., Myklebust, H. (1967) *Learning Disabilities: Educational Principles and Practices.* New York: Grune & Stratton.

Kaufman, A. (1979) *Intelligent Testing with the WISC-R.* New York: John Wiley & Sons.

Killen, J. (1975) A Learning Systems Approach to Intervention. In *Progress in Learning Disabilities, Volume 111,* Editor: Helmer Myklebust. New York: Grune & Stratton, Inc.

Kinsbourne, M. (1972: 176, 539-541) Eye and head turning indicates cerebral lateralization. *Science*

Lefevre, E., Starck, R., Lambert, W.E., and Genesee, F. (1977: 44, 1115-1122) Lateral eye movements during verbal and nonverbal dichotic listening. *Perceptual and Motor Skills.*

Loehr, J. (1982) *Athletic Excellence: Mental Toughness in Sports.* Denver: Forum.

Mischel, Walter. (1981) Metacognition and the rules of delay. In *Social Cognitive Development: Frontiers and Possible Futures.* J.H. Flavell & L. Ross (Editors). New York: Cambridge University Press.

Myklebust, H. (1965) *Development and Disorders of Written Language: Picture Story Language Test, Volume 1.* New York: Grune & Stratton, Inc.

Myklebust, H., Bannochie, M., & Killen, J. (1971) Learning Disabilities and Cognitive Processes. In *Progress in Learning Disabilities, Volume 11.* Editor: Helmer Myklebust. New York: Grune & Stratton, Inc.

Rourke, B., Fisk, J., & Strang, J. (1986) *Neuropsychological Assessment of Children: A Treatment Oriented Approach.* New York: The Guildford Press.

Sereda, Andrew. (1987) *Headache Control Without Drugs: New Concepts in the Prevention and Treatment of Nervous System Symptoms and Illness.* Edmonton: Amaranthine Press.

CHAPTER 4

Bloom, B.S., Engelhart, M.D., Furst, E.J., Hill, W.H., and Krathwohl, D.R. (Eds.) (1956) *Taxonomy of Educational Objectives: The Classification of Educational Goals. Handbook 1: Cognitive Domain.* New York: David McKay Company, Inc.

Boder, E. (1971) Developmental Dyslexia: Prevailing Diagnostic Concepts and a New Diagnostic Approach. In *Progress in Learning Disabilities.* Ed. H.R. Myklebust. New York: Grune & Stratton.

Brookes, Mona, (1986) *Drawing with Children: A Creative Teaching and Learning Method That Works for Adults, Too.* Los Angeles: Jeremy P. Teacher, Inc.

Bry, A. (1978) *Visualizing: Directing the Movies of your Mind.* New York: Barnes & Noble Books.

Chall, J.S., & Mirsky, A.F. (1978) *Education And The Brain: The Seventy-seventh Yearbook of the National Society for the Study of Education*. Chicago, Illinois: The University of Chicago Press.

DeMille, R. (1979) *Put Your Mother On The Ceiling: Children's Imagination Games*. New York: Penguin Books.

Feuerstein, (1980) *Instrumental Enrichment: An Intervention Program for Cognitive Modifiability*. Baltimore, University Press.

Flaro, L. ((1986: 15, 2, 18-23) An Evaluation of the NLP Spelling Strategy with Learning Disabled Students. *Teaching Atypical Students in Alberta*.

Flaro, L. (winter 1987/88) The Development and Evaluation of a Reading Comprehension Strategy with Learning Disabled Students. *Reading Improvement: Journal for the Improvement of Reading Teaching*.

Flaro, L. Eye Movement Patterns, Cognitive Systems and Verbal-Performance Discrepancies on the WISC-R. In Preparation.

Gur, R.E., Gur, R.C., & Marshalek, B. (1975: 67, 151- 153) Classroom seating and functional brain asymmetry. *Journal of Educational Psychology*.

Hershey, M. (1979: 23, 1, 71-77) The Effect of Guided Fantasy on the Creative Writing Ability of Gifted Students. *The Gifted Child Quarterly*.

Houston, Jean. (1982) The Possible Human. Los Angeles: J.P.Tarcher, Inc.

Kane, M. & Kane, N. (1979: 23, 1, 157-167) Comparison of R/L Hemisphere Functions. *The Gifted Child Quarterly*.

Khatena, J. (1979: 23, 4, 735-747) Nurture of Imagery in the Visual Performing Arts. *The Gifted Child Quarterly*.

Kinsbourne, M. (1972: 176, 539-541) Eye and Head Turning Indicates Cerebral Lateralization. *Science*.

Kinsbourne, (1974:12, 279 - 281) Direction of Eye Gaze and Distribution of Cerebral Thought Processes. *Neuropschologia*.

Levy, J., & Reid, M. (1976: 194, 337-339) Variations in writing posture and cerebral organizations. *Science*.

Levy, J., & Reid, M. (1978: 107, 119-144) Variations in cerebral organization as a function of handedness, hand posture in writing, and sex. *Journal of Experimental Psychology: General*.

Lowenfels, Manna. (1979: 23, 4, 801 -806) Releasing Creativity through Image-Making. *The Gifted Child Quarterly*.

Markoff, A.M. (1976) *Teaching Low-Achieving Children Reading, Spelling and Handwriting: Developing Perceptual Skills With The Graphic Symbols of Language*. Springfield, Illinois: Charles C. Thomas Publisher.

McKim, R.H. (1972) *Experiences in Visual Thinking*. Monterey California: Brooks/Coles.

Moscovitch, M., & Smith, L.C. (1976: 205, 710-713) Differences in neural organization between individuals with inverted and noninverted handwriting postures. *Science*.

Mykelbust, H.R. (1965) *Development and Disorders of Written Language, Volume 1*. New York: Grune & Stratton.

Myklebust, H.R. (1978) Toward a Science of Dyslexiology. In *Progress in Learning Disabilities, Volume 1V*. New York: Grune & Stratton.

Morton, L.L. & Kershner, J.R. (1987: 6, 101-111) Hemisphere Asymmetries, Spelling Ability, and Classroom Seating in Fourth Graders. *Brain and Cognition*.

Nelson, H.E., & Warrington, E.K. (1976: 325-332) Developmental spelling retardation. In Knights, R.M. & Bakker, D.J. (Eds). *The Neuropsychology of Learning Disorders.* Baltimore: University Park Press.

Prichard, Allyn. (1980) *Accelerating Learning: The Use of Suggestion in the Classroom.* Novato, California: Academic Therapy Publications.

Reitan, R.M. (1984) *Aphasis and Sensory Perceptual Deficits in Children.* Tucson, Arizona: Neuropsychology Press.

Rourke, B.P. (1985) *Neuropsychology of Learning Disabilities: Essentials of Subtype Analysis.* New York: The Guildford Press.

Rourke, B.P., Bakker, D.J., Fisk, J.L., & Strang, J.D., (1983) *Child Neuropsychology: An Indroduction to Theory, Research, and Clinical Practice.* New York: The Guildford Press.

Rourke, B.P., & Finlayson, M.A.J. (1978: 6, 121-133) Neuropsychological significance of variations in patterns of academic performance: Verbal and visualspatial abilities. *Journal of Abnormal Child Psychology.*

Rourke, B.P. & Strang, J.D. (1978: 2, 62-66) Neuropsychological significance of variations in patterns of academicjperformance: Motor, psychomotor, tactile-perceptual abilities. *Journal of Pediatric Psychology.*

Schroeder, N. (1976: 42, 865-866) Lateral eye shift related to preschoolers use of descriptive language. *Perceptual Medicine.*

Strang, J.D., & Rourke, B.P. (1983: 12, 33-39) Concept-Formation/non-verbal reasoning abilities of children who exhibit specific academic problems with arithmetic. *Journal of Clinical Child Psychology.*

Sweeny, J.E. & Rourke, B.P. (1978: 6, 212-225) Neuropsychological significance of phonetically accurate and phonetically inaccurate spelling errors in younger and older retarded spellers. *Brain and Language.*

Wittrock, M.C. (1978) Education and the Cognitive Processes of the Brain. In *Education and the Brain: The Seventy-senventh Yearbook of the National Society for the Study of Education.* J.S. Chall & A. F. Mirsky (Eds.) Chicago, Illinois: The University of Chicago Press.

CHAPTER 5

Ackerman, P.T., Anhalt, J.M. & Dykman, R.A. (1986,April: 19, 4, 222-232) Arithmetic Automatization Failure with Attention and Reading Disorders: Associations and Sequela. *Journal of Learning Disabilities.*

Bayliss, J. & Livesey, P.J. (1985, June/July: 18, 326-332) Cognitive Strategies of Children with Reading Disability and Normal Readers in Visual Sequential Memory. *Journal of Learning Disabilities.*

Bettelheim, B., & Zelan, K. (1982) *On Learning to Read.* New York: Vintage Books.

Brailsford, A., Snart, F. & Das, J.P. (1984, May: 17, 287 290) Strategy Training and Reading Comprehension. *Journal of Learning Disabilities.*

Carroll, J.B. (1972) Defining language comprehension: Some speculations. In J.B. Corroll & R. O. Freedle (Eds.) *Language comprehension and the acquisition of knowledge.*

Das, J.P., Kirby, J. & Jarman, R. (1979) *Simultaneous and Successive Cognitive Processing.* New York: Academic Press.

Das, J.P., Snart, F. & Mulcahy, R.F. (1982) *Reading Disability and Its Relation to Information Integration, In Theory and Research In Learning Disabilities.* Eds. J.P. Das, R.F. Mulcahy and A.E.Wall. New York: Plenum Press.

Farnham-Diggory, (1968) *Learning Disabilities* Massachusetts: Harvard University Press.

Golinkoff, R.M. (1975/76: 4, 623-659) A comparison of reading comprehension processes in good and poor comprehenders. *Reading Research Quarterly.*

Gordon, & Poze, (1979) Learning Dysfunction and Connection Making. *In The Metaphorical Way of Learning and Knowing* Cambridge: SES Associates.

Gordon, (1978) *Therapeutic Metaphors* META Publications. Cupertino California.

Irwin, J.W. (1986) *Teaching Reading Comprehension Processes.* Englewood Cliffs, New Jersey: Prentice Hall, Inc.

Kaufman, (1980) Kaufman Assessment Battery for Children: Interpretive Manual. Circle Pines, Minnesota: American Guidance Service, Inc.

Leong, Che Kan, (1982) Promising Areas of Research into Learning Disabilities with Emphasis on Reading Disabilities. In *Theory And Research In Learning Disabilities.* Eds. J.P. Das, R.F. Mulcahy, and A.E. Wall. New York: Plenum Press.

Levine, M. Brooks, R. Shonoff, J. *A Pediatric Approach to Learning Disorders* New York: John Wiley & Sons.

Meichenbaum, (1977) *Cognitive-Behavior Modification: An Integrative Approach* New York: Plenum Press.

Mills & Crowley, (1986) *Therapeutic Metaphors for Children and the Child Within* New York: Brunner/Mazel.

Nagel, C.V., Reese, E. Reese, M. & Suidzinski, R. (1985) *Megateaching and Learning: Neurolinguistic Programming Applied to Education.* Indian Rock Beach: Southern Institute Press.

Paivio, A (1971) *Imagery and Verbal Proceses* New York: Holt.

Polya, (1945) *How to Solve It* New Jersey Princeton University Press.

Pressley, M. (1976: 68, 355 -359) Mental Imagery helps eight year olds remember what they read. *Journal of Educational Psychology*

Samuels, S.J. & Eisenberg, P. (1981) A Framework For

Understanding The Reading Process. In *Neuropsychological And Cognitive Processes in Reading.* F.J. Pirozzolo & M.C. Wittrock (Eds). New York: Academic Press.

Slade, P.D., & Russell, G.F. (1971: 1, 292-298) Developmental dyscalulia: A brief report on four cases. *Psychological Medicine.*

Spiro, R.J., Bruce, C., & Brewer, W.F. (1980) *Theoretical Issues in Reading Comprehension.* Hillsdale, New Jersey: Lawrence Erlbaum.

Strang, J.D. & Rourke, B.P. (1985) Arithmetic Disability Subtypes: The Neuropsychological Significance of Specific Arithmetical Impairment in Childhood. In *Neuropsychololgy of Learning Disabilities: Essentials of Subtype Analysis.* B.P. Rourke (Ed.) New York: The Guildford Press.

Torgesen, J., & Kail, R., (1980) Memory processes in exceptional children, chapter in *Advances in Special Education; Volume 1: Basic Constructs and Theoretical Orientations, a Research Annual.* B.K. Keogh (Ed). Greenwich, Connecticut: JAI Press.

Tuoko, H. (1982); Cognitive correlates of arithmetic performance in clinic referred children. Unpublished doctoral dissertation, University of Victoria.

Vellutino & Scanlon, (1982: 14) Development and Evaluation of Reading Comprehension.

Walberg, (1980)

Wittrock, M.C. (1981) Reading Comprehension. In *Neuropsychological And Cognitive Processes in Reading.* F.J. Pitozzolo & M.C. Wittrock. (Eds). New York: Academic Press.

CHAPTER 6

Almy, M. (1970: 61-75) New Views on Intellectual Development in Early Childhood Education. In *Educational Implications of Paiget's Theory,* I.J. Athey & D.O. Rubadeau, (Eds). Waltham, Massachussets: Xerox College Publishing.

Bandler, R. & Grinder, J. (1979) *Frogs into Princes: Neurolinguistic Programming.* Maob, Utah: Real People Press.

Bruner, Jerome et al. (1966) *Studies in Cognitive Growth* New York: John Wiley & Sons, Inc.

Dilts, Robert et al.(1980) *Neuro-linguistic Programming: The Study of Structure of Subjective Experience.* Cupertino, California.

Flavell, J. (1963) *The Developmental Psychology of John Piaget* New York: D. Van Nostrand Company.

Gaddes, W.H. (1980) *Learning Disabilities and Brain Function: A Neuropsychological Approach.* New York: Springer-Verlag.

Gardner, Howard. (1983) *Frames of Mind: The Theory of Multiple Intelligence.* New York: Basic Books, Inc., Publishers.

Johnson, D.J. & Myklebust, H.R. (1967) *Learning Disabilities: Educational Principles and Practices.* New York: Grune & Stratton.

Kaufman, A. (1979) *Intelligent Testing With the WISC-R.* New York: John Wiley & Sons.

Korzybski, Alfred. (1973) *Science and Sanity.* Clinton, Massachussets: The Colonial Press, Inc.

Lankton, S.R. & Lankton, C.H. (1983) *The Answer Within: A Clinical Framework of Ericksonian Hypnotherapy.* New York: Bruner/Mazel Publishers.

Luria, A.R. (1973) *The Working Brain.* Middlesex, England: Penguin Books.

Montessori, Maria, (1967) *The Absorbent Mind.* New York: Dell Publishing Company, Inc.

Ross, A. (1980) *Learning Disability: The Unrealized Potential* New York: McGraw Hill.

Rourke, B., Bakker, D.J., Fisk, J. & Strang, J. (1983) *Child Neuropsychology.* New York: The Guildford Press.

Rourke, B., (Ed) (1985) *Neuropsychology of Learning Disabilities: Essentials of Subtype Analysis.* New York: The Guildford Press.

Sattler, J.M. (1982) *Assessment of Children's Intelligence and Special Abilities.* Boston: Alun and Bacon, Inc.

John-Steiner, Vera, (1985) *Notebooks of the Mind: Explorations of Thinking.* New York: Harper & Row, Publishers.

Watzlawick, P., Weakland, John & Fisch, R. (1974) Change: *Principles of Problem Formation and Problem Resolution.* New York: W.W. Norton & Company, Inc.

INDEX